CONTROL THE ROCK

Lessons My Dad Taught Me About
Pool, Courage, and Life

MANUEL GONZALES III
WITH RICK KILLIAN

MEDIA.COM

Control the Rock
Copyright © 2024 by Manuel Gonzales III

All rights reserved. No part of this book may be reproduced in any form or by any means—whether electronic, digital, mechanical, or otherwise—without permission in writing from the publisher, except by a reviewer, who may quote brief passages in a review. The views and opinions expressed in this book are those of the author and do not necessarily reflect the official policy or position of Illumify Media Global.

Published by

Illumify Media Global

www.IllumifyMedia.com

"Let's bring your book to life!"

Library of Congress Control Number: 2024914915

Paperback ISBN: 978-1-964251-13-4

Manuscript prepared in collaboration with Rick Killian, Killian Creative, Boulder, Colorado. www.killiancreative.com

Cover design by Debbie Lewis

Printed in the United States of America

Contents

1	Control the Rock	1
2	The Cue Ball Doesn't Lie	23
3	Play the Table	41
4	Begin with Victory in Mind	57
5	Limitations Aren't Always Limitations	75
6	Tinker with Intent	95
7	Courage	117
8	Respect Yourself and Others	137
9	Why We Play	161
10	Be a Teacher	181
11	Live Gracefully	203
12	Never Give Up	223

From the VNEA Hall of Fame Website 242

Notes 245

About the Author 247

To Dad and Mom

You saved each other and built a life together
that touched so many lives.

We will be forever grateful.

Me and my dad

ONE

Control the Rock

> The game of pool begins with controlling "the rock"—making the cue ball do exactly what you want it to do. If you can't control the cue ball, you're relying on luck more than skill. The game begins with figuring out what you want the cue ball to do—beginning, middle, and end of the shot.
> —Manuel Gonzales Jr.

Like me, and like my oldest son after me, my dad fell in love with playing pool from watching his dad play pool. I have no idea how good my grandfather was, but it is obvious he loved the game enough to play it often, and when they were old enough—probably five or six—he took my dad and my Uncle Leo with him, like my dad first took me and like I took my oldest son as soon as he was tall enough to see over the rail and hold a cue stick by himself.

What I know about pool—and life—I learned pretty much from watching my dad, talking with him, or having him show me. Over the years, I've found, time and again, that his lessons have been wisdom worth following.

My dad said my grandfather was pretty good. But then, every twelve-year-old kid probably thinks his dad is good at everything. I say twelve because that's the age my dad was the last time he saw my grandfather play. That's how old he was when my grandfather died. How my grandfather died is still a mystery to this day.

I can't imagine what that was like for my dad, and he never really talked about it. Nor has he ever spoken with me about how he lost part of his arm and a leg while in Vietnam. Neither my oldest sister, Denise, nor my older sister, Renee, nor I ever asked him about it while we were growing up. It was a subject too sensitive to be explored with him. But we didn't need to know either. To us, he was amazing, and we were blessed to have him as our dad. We were the lucky ones. It wasn't until we got much older that he started to open up a little, but conversations about his war years always ended with him near tears and asking if he could have a little time to himself.

As I got older and more curious, I realized he was only comfortable talking about the war with other veterans who had been there. I would eavesdrop on those conversations when the opportunity came along, but I never came away with my biggest question answered: How did he get hurt? Slowly over the years—as he spoke with more veterans or was interviewed by the local newspaper, the *Greeley Tribune*—

I learned more, but for years I only learned bits and pieces.

I can't say that I blame him for not wanting to revisit those memories, though. In fact, it created in me a greater love and respect for him than words can express. He was never a man to opt for violence or anger to solve a problem. He was a man of courage and peace through and through.

But that didn't mean he wouldn't give you a good beating on the pool table if he had a chance. There he ruled with precision and friendliness. Pretty good for a man with only one arm and one leg. It wasn't about the competition, though; it was about the art.

At his prime, Dad was one of the best pool players in the state of Colorado—even in the United States, really. He was the toughest, kindest person I've ever known. Not only did he lose an arm and a leg, but it was his right hand he lost, and he grew up right-handed, so he had to learn to play with his left. He overcame all of that to play the game he loved—and to do much more. I grew up with him overcoming any and every obstacle in front of him. Writing with his left hand, jumping on a trampoline, driving a car, working on cars, repairing VCRs and other electronics in his workshop, and so many other tasks. He was so good at these things that it wasn't until I was much older that I ever considered how difficult that must've been for him.

In watching him compete in tournaments—in watching how he never acted like any of his injuries mattered or held him back in any way—I learned about courage.

As you might imagine, my dad stuck out wherever he went. When we were younger, my sisters and I would notice how people would stare at him, especially kids. My sisters and I would handle the situation differently. If I noticed a kid staring at him, it would make me smile. I understood their curiosity. It would cause me to hang on to my dad a little tighter, knowing how amazing he was and how lucky I felt that he was my dad.

My sister Denise would get protective. She would stare them down and have to refrain from saying anything. She would hang on to him tight and say to herself, *This is my dad*. I understand now how her love for him created that response.

My sister Renee would handle it somewhere in between. She would make sure that they knew she saw them staring, but she also understood their curiosity.

Dad especially stood out in pool halls. It's not often you see a guy with only one arm and one leg playing pool. In fact, in all my years of playing, my dad was the only person like that I've ever seen play. And then, on top of that, he was good. *Really* good. He won a lot of matches and several of the tournaments he entered. Anyone who played him and thought maybe they should take it easy on him quickly learned better than to underestimate him. It was a mistake they didn't make twice.

Dad always drew a crowd too. He was fascinating to watch. The way he balanced on one leg with his crutch and eyed the ball, lining up his pool cue as it rested on a specially designed bridge he carried in a little slot in his crutch or a small beanbag he always carried with him on the rail, all seemed so impossible. And then the shots he would make! Kevin Silverberg, a good friend of Dad's he used to play with a lot, once told me of a shot Dad made in a nine-ball tournament. Dad lined up on a long straight-in shot, but to get position on the next ball required a very controlled long draw stroke. He executed it perfectly, and then proceeded to run out the rack. One of the younger guys in the tournament came up to him after that and held up his cue with both hands. "Mister," he asked, "can you make my cue do that?"

Dad looked at him, a little embarrassed, and smiled. "Just practice. You can do it too."

The Four Manuels

My grandfather's name—the man my dad grew up watching—was Manuel Gonzales, and he named my father after himself. Growing up, even though my grandfather wasn't around, my dad always went by Manuel Jr.—or Manny to his friends. As his oldest son, I was given the name Manuel as well, which made me Manuel Gonzales III. When I started playing in the tournaments, I would write

"Manuel Gonzales" as my name and Dad would write "Manuel Gonzales Jr." When people would look at the tournament bracket, they would get us confused, thinking "Manuel Gonzales" was the father and "Manuel Jr." was the son. Players would show up at the table expecting my dad but playing me, or vice versa.

Manuel Sr. and Manuel Jr.

One time we were playing some mini tournaments to warm up for a regular tournament, and I got to play Colorado's top player at the time, Melvin "The Black Rattlesnake" Sharp, and I beat him. Then we played again in another warm-up, and I beat him again. When Melvin went to sign up for another warm-up mini tournament and saw he would be paired with Manuel Jr., he hesitated. Dad was there, though, and told him, "No, that's not my son, that's me," so he signed up. Then my dad drew him in the first round, and my dad beat him. Dad and I had some pretty good laughs about that one in the years that followed.

It wasn't long before I was dubbed "MG3" to clear things up. My oldest son, Manuel Gonzales IV, also entered quite a few tournaments with my dad and had similar experiences, so to help with any confusion, he was quickly nicknamed "MG4." (My son, by the way, does everything right-handed but play pool, which he plays left-handed from growing up watching and learning from his granddad.)

Growing up, I never thought much about my dad having only one arm and leg—especially that it could be a disadvantage playing pool—until I found some old clippings of newspaper articles from the *Greeley Tribune*. They wrote about him as a pool champion. They also commemorated him as a decorated veteran who was a local boy who'd gone off one mid-July day in 1967 to fight in Vietnam. The first part I knew well; the second it would take me until the months just before he passed away to uncover in more detail.

Dad taught me about life; he taught me the importance of faith; he taught me again and again about how to be an entrepreneur before anyone really used the word. Anything I have done right in business over the years, I feel like I did either because I was emulating him or because of a principle he taught me. When we wanted to have fun, he taught me how to play pool. That, in turn, turned me into a pool champion in my own right. You can't go to any pool hall in northern Colorado and not find someone who knows the name Manuel Gonzales, whether that be II, III, or IV.

But more than anything, Dad taught me how to face down difficulties and challenges with grace. He taught me how to beat the odds. The courage with which he faced life was something I've tried to live up to. The things he said over and over teaching me how to play pool and live with courage still ring in my ears. The only thing I could think to do with them was write them down and share them with my family, his friends, and anyone interested in picking up a pool cue and trying to knock balls into pockets. They are all worth remembering.

Pool—and Life—in One Principle

When my dad taught people how to play pool, he always started in the same place: their base.

He knew proper mechanics were key to controlling the cue ball, and whenever you were struggling, it was time to go back to the basics. Proper mechanics include where you set your feet (your stance), how you drop down on the ball to sight along the pool cue to find your aim-line, where and how you grip the pool cue, your stroke, staying down during and after the shot, and your follow-through.

Pool is all about "controlling the rock"—i.e., the cue ball. Everything else is secondary. Following Newton's third law of motion—"for every action there is an equal and opposite reaction"—the game is played by hitting the cue ball with the right amount of force and spin so that it affects the object balls the way you would like and comes to a stop to set up your next shot. A sloppy approach to controlling the cue ball will result in sloppy play. You've got to control the rock to win.

Dad always said that in the game of pool—like in life—there are only so many things you can control. In poker, they say it's all about "how well you play the cards you're dealt." In pool, it's all about how well you play the table as it lies before you. The only shot you ever really get that is the same is the break. The rest is you making the right choices for the layout of the balls on the table before you. Once you choose the ball you're aiming to sink, then your personal skills and talent come into play. And both of those depend on you making the cue ball do exactly what you want it to do, so that the rest of the balls do what you want as well.

My dad didn't come into the world with many advantages. He was born to migrant farmer workers in Woodland, California. His older brother, my Uncle Leo, was born the year before somewhere in Utah. My grandparents were both young at the time. Grandpa Manuel and Grandma Mary were married when he was seventeen and she was eighteen, on April 28, 1947. My dad was born seventeen months later, before either of them was twenty. After having my dad, it seems like Grandpa had earned enough money to settle down in one place. The family moved to Denver not long after that, where three of my aunts and my Uncle Robert were born.

Mary and Manuel Sr., my grandparents

My dad remembered Grandma Mary—whose maiden name was Pisano—as a great cook. Her mother died when she was young, so as the oldest daughter, it was up to her to raise her brothers and sisters. I remember when I was younger that she had a reputation for making the best tamales in town. When I was six or seven, she would take me with her selling them door to door. Maybe that's where my dad got his entrepreneurial spirit.

Her dad, my Great-grandfather Ecidro Pisano, owned a farm in Greeley, a small town in the flatlands of eastern Colorado about an hour north of Denver and an hour east of the Rocky Mountains. That is where my grandparents were married. They immediately started traveling to wherever they could find field work, which is how they ended up in Utah when Uncle Leo was born.

During the 1920s, Denver was a growing city, and its oldest neighborhood, Auraria, held a thriving Hispanic community. Auraria was actually there before Denver. *Auraria* means "gold" in Latin, expressing the hope of its earliest settlers. (Colorado's gold rush was very, very brief, though—there was more silver and coal found.) After World War I, Hispanic servicemen and Mexican immigrants moved to Auraria for the factory and agricultural jobs.[1] That's where my grandparents settled after Dad was born.

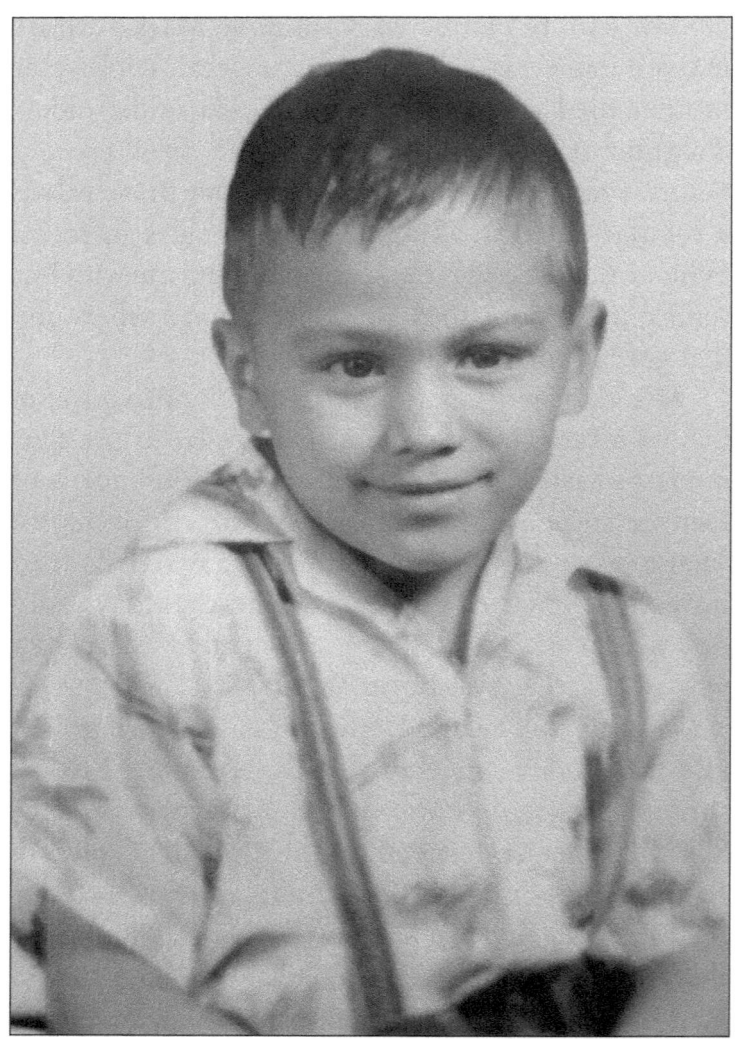

Manuel Jr., my dad

According to Dad, when he was very young, they lived in two different houses in the Auraria neighborhood, the first near the Tivoli Brewery and not far from Casa Mayan, the first Mexican restaurant in Denver. Today, the buildings in that area that were not protected for their historic value are gone. Many were torn down after severe flooding in 1965, when it was decided to turn the area into a home for three college campuses: Metro State University, University of Colorado at Denver, and the Community College of Denver.[2] Casa Mayan is now administrative offices, and the old Tivoli building is the Tivoli Student Union. Tivoli Brewery opened again in 2015 and is housed in the original brewing area of the Student Union. The building was originally constructed in 1864 near Colorado's first artesian well.

When Dad was about seven, they moved north to the projects off Federal Boulevard, where he later went to junior high. Uncle Donnie, Dad's godfather, moved in with them for a time. There was always room for family in those days. Dad remembered, while they lived there, his grandpa (Grandma Mary's father) would bring him up to Greeley, and Dad would work irrigating his farm and doing other chores during the spring and summer. In exchange for his help, Great-Grandpa Pisano would buy Dad some new clothes and supplies for school.

Grandma Mary's sister, Natalie, was Dad's godmother, and her family lived nearby in Denver as well. When Dad was young, she used to make lemon meringue pies that were a favorite of the family. Dad said Uncle Leo used to always try to get Dad's piece in addition to his own! Unfortunately, Aunt Natalie died during childbirth when Dad and Uncle Leo were still young.

My dad and Uncle Leo

As one of his first jobs, Uncle Leo worked with some friends at Bears Stadium at Twentieth and Clay, where the Denver Bears baseball team played. (That stadium was eventually turned into Mile High Stadium and shared with the Denver Broncos.) The Bears became the Zephyrs in 1955 and relocated to New Orleans when the Rockies were formed in

1993. Grandpa used to take Dad and Uncle Leo to Bears games when he could.

At one point, the Bears had a raffle, but anyone who worked at the stadium wasn't eligible to enter, so Uncle Leo and his friends talked Dad into entering. The first prize was a pony, and the third prize was five hundred dollars. Together they all agreed that if Dad won the first prize, they would sell the pony, and the same with the second prize (he couldn't remember what it was). They would use the money to buy them all baseball gear: gloves, bats, hats, etc.

As things would have it, Dad won the five-hundred-dollar third prize, and he and Uncle Leo took the money to Grandpa and told him what they had agreed to do with it. Grandpa took the money and bought the equipment for them, but that didn't use up all the money. With the boys' permission, he took the rest and used it as a down payment on a car, which was the first car Dad remembers the family owning.

When Uncle Leo's boss heard that they had won the money, he went to my grandpa and threatened to report to the Bears organization that Dad worked for them unless Grandpa gave him some of it. He thought, given the circumstances, he could intimidate Grandpa into giving him a cut. Instead of backing down, though, Grandpa called his bluff. It's not sure what words were exchanged or how he managed to turn the tables on him, but Grandpa stood his ground and refused to give him anything. In the end, the guy never said anything to anyone about it, so Grandpa must have been pretty persuasive.

As I mentioned before, one of Grandpa Manuel's favorite pastimes was playing pool, and he used to take Dad and Uncle Leo with him when he went to play, leaving their mother and three sisters—Mary Helen, Pauline, and Kathy—at home. They started out playing pinball while Grandpa played pool, but pretty soon they got interested in watching and then wanted to play themselves, so Grandpa gave them money to play on the pool table next to his. Dad said Uncle Leo, being taller, took to the game faster than he did. For a time, they watched Grandpa play, and then they would wait for him to finish so they could go home. Eventually it was Grandpa who was waiting for them.

In those days, and even when I was growing up, the pool halls weren't a bad place for kids to hang out, especially if their dads were with them. Sure, there was a small amount of gambling and drinking, but pool players worth their salt didn't overindulge if they wanted to stay competitive. The pool halls were places where there were regulars who looked out for each other and where skill was appreciated. It was something of a community.

The pursuit of excellence was in the air and was caught by anyone who picked up a pool cue. There was no formal teaching per se, but players were free with advice, and there were good players to watch and imitate. Money games drew spectators, even if rarely over a dozen people. When they were younger, winnings were small—often only pocket change. They played for money lots of times. Dad said they used to play pea ball on the snooker table for quarters or fifty cents at Sportsman's when he was in his teens.

Uncle Leo, in particular, had a knack for money games. It was easier than earning money working in the fields, after all. Sometimes pots were as much as ten or twenty dollars if someone with deep pockets was around, which was a considerable amount back in the '50s and early '60s. They rarely went home with less money than they'd come with.

The 1960s began with the birth of my Uncle Robert, then ended with a tragic turn for Dad's family. My grandfather died on December 10, 1960. I can hardly imagine what it was like for my Grandma Mary to have six children, one still under a year old, and be on her own. I imagine my dad got his strength from her.

Shrinking Your Game

In his book *The One Thing*, Gary Keller discusses how we tend to think there are so many requirements in life and success comes from meeting them all, when in fact there is often just one critical thing that needs to be done that will make all the difference to meet the next big goal. In pool a similar thing happens with beginning players. They get overwhelmed by the number of balls and options on the table and how they are going to sink them, when what they really need to do is leave that to focus first on one thing. They need to find one pattern of shots through the chaos, then focus on what they need the cue ball to do, then determine which is the best way to hit their first shot to set themselves up for their second and third.

The most successful athletes are often the ones who can do something similar to this—they are able to block out what has happened before and what they hope will happen by the end and focus on the one thing they need to do for the next play. Baseball pitchers turn nine innings into dozens of smaller games of one pitch versus one batter at a time. Each throw becomes their sole focus, and the most important thing is making the baseball do exactly what they want it to do on the next delivery to the plate. Once that is done, they start all over. The fact that the last pitch might have hit a batter or was knocked over the fence for a home run doesn't matter. It's all about stringing the upcoming throws together to create outs and not runs.

In his book, Keller calls this "going small." The key is to focus on achievement more than productivity. As he puts it, "The answer is making the heart of things the heart of their approach. They go small."[3] Rather than focusing on getting everything on their to-do list checked off, they focus on getting the next most important thing done well.

Keller learned this as he coached agents in his organization, Keller Real Estate. Initially, he'd end calls with them by listing a handful of things they should do before their next call together. What he found was that most of them would get most of the tasks accomplished but not really be that much better off for their efforts. In fact, they tended to avoid the most important task for ones that were easier to accomplish. As a result, they weren't making real progress. They weren't doing the things on the list that mattered most. So he began limiting their to-dos to three things. A bit better, but not much. Then two. Same. Then, out of desperation, he began helping them identify the one key thing they could do in the next week that would make the biggest difference.

Boom!

Massive improvements.

As he put it, this came from ignoring what you *could* do and determining what you *should* do. Not every task checked off a list would have the same weight in moving the needle on success. There had to be a tighter focus on the desired outcomes and goals. He discovered that "extraordinary results are directly determined by how narrow you can make your focus."[4]

In pool, this is even more important. You've got to control the rock, which means learning how to send the cue ball on a specific path by choosing the right speed, aim-line, and English (or spin), and then executing the shot with precise cueing. It's not about sinking the easiest shot on the table, but about sinking the ball, that will make the next shots easier—or at least possible—to pocket.

In the movie *For the Love of the Game*, Kevin Costner plays a veteran pitcher on the edge of retirement, probably playing in his last game. Wanting to give his best performance, at the beginning of every inning, as is his routine, he stands on the mound taking in the excitement of the crowd and the beauty of the day. Then he speaks three words to himself: "Clear the mechanism." At this, the crowd noise is silenced, and everything is shut out besides the sixty feet and six inches between himself and home plate. He reduces the entire game down to throwing one ball and having it hit the exact spot he wants with the right amount of movement.

Later in the game, as he begins to fatigue, the catcher, played by John C. Reilly, comes to the mound, and Costner asks him, looking around at the ballpark, "Anybody been on base?"

"Nobody," Reilly answers.

"Nobody?"

"This I ain't seen much of. Huh."

"Me neither."[5]

He had been so focused on throwing each pitch, he didn't realize he was on the edge of a perfect game.

It's that same kind of focus my dad taught me to have in pool—to shrink the entire game down to the next three shots, and then further down to the one point on the cue ball I had to hit. If I could do that, good things would follow.

Every other success in pool is decided by doing that one thing over and over again. String enough successes together, and good things happen again and again.

In Life, as in Pool

I can't imagine my dad's circumstances growing up were easy, but as he used to say, you play the table as it lies. You don't get to rearrange the balls to make things easier; you have to play the balls where they are, obstacles and all.

The thing is, no matter where you are in life, there are difficulties, but you have choices. You can see these things as prejudices and hardships—injustices set against you—and if you do, it's easy to let them get the best of you. In pool, balls will cluster together making it hard to get a clear pattern. Some will be in your way, some will be pressed up against the rails, and others will be scattered at awkward angles. It can look like chaos. You can see it as bad luck, you can see the odds that are stacked against you, or you can see the opportunities. You can wish for better circumstances, or you can practice to be ready for the most difficult challenges.

And that's where the artistry is. When you can make the difficult look easy, when you can creatively solve complicated problems, that's when the game gets fun, and that's when consistently winning comes within your grasp. I saw my dad do this time and again on the pool table with everything stacked against him, and I saw him do it in life, when people either wanted to feel sorry for him or look down on him for one reason or another. He heard a lot of "You can'ts" in his life, but he always found a way.

The principle translates throughout life. In pool, you focus on the cue ball and what you must make it do both to succeed at the present shot and to set you up to make the next. In life, you have to discern from all the chaos what the one next best thing is for you to do and do it well. That's how you win. You've got to control the rock—you've got to *be* the rock. You've got to be someone who makes good things happen.

TWO

The Cue Ball Doesn't Lie

> The balls on the table will always react the same way, depending on how you hit the cue ball. If you don't get the reaction you wanted, then go back and look at how you hit the cue ball. The cue ball doesn't lie—it will always tell you how you actually hit it, not how you thought you hit it.
> —Manuel Gonzales Jr.

Within a few years of Grandpa Manuel's death, Grandma Mary married Oscar Santos, who was better known as "Sammy." They had two daughters together, my Aunt Irene on February 21, 1962, and my Aunt Theresa on January 19, 1963. They were both born in Denver.

Sammy was a field worker from Texas, and the family all lived together for a time in a big white house on Spring Street in Denver. Neither the house nor Spring Street still exist, probably casualties of the big South Platte River flood in the spring of 1965 that wiped out most of the Auraria neighborhoods.

The floods came when fourteen inches of rain fell on Dawson Butte in about four hours, cutting new channels into the butte's steep slopes and overwhelming the gullies, streams, and South Platte downstream. The flood claimed twenty-one lives and resulted in an estimated $543 million of property damage. Dad once told me the house they lived in was across the street from the Green Lantern Bar (which I can also find no record of) and that there were three bars right next to each other all in that same area. Luckily, they weren't living in Denver in 1965 to see it all get wiped out.

Instead, soon after Aunt Theresa was born, Sammy talked Grandma into moving the family to O'Donnell, Texas, which was closer to Sammy's family, who lived just across the border from El Paso in Juárez, Mexico. They lived between O'Donnell and Juárez for about a year and a half. Dad went to school in O'Donnell for a year. He would have been fourteen or fifteen. They went back and forth to "Old Mexico" often, living there for about six months at one point.

Dad thought it was fabulous in Juárez. He and Uncle Leo were popular because they were fluent in both Spanish and English and could talk with anyone, as well as help translate. It was during one of their visits to Sammy's parents that John F. Kennedy was assassinated in Dallas, which was only about a ten-hour drive away. Dad remembered that vividly because they couldn't get back into the United States most of the day. The border was closed as soon as the assassination took place, and it remained closed for six hours, until after the main suspect, Lee Harvey Oswald, was taken into custody.[6] Even then, only American citizens with proper identification were allowed to cross into El Paso.

During the time they were living in Old Mexico, Dad got a job working for one of Sammy's cousins repairing tires in his "shop," which was little more than an old shack with a dirt floor, a tire machine, and some other miscellaneous tools. Dad worked there with Sammy's little brother, and they would ride the bus together to get there from Sammy's parents' house.

It was while living there that Dad realized he had a knack for working with engines and repairing machines. He just seemed to understand how parts went together. One time, one of Sammy's cousins was working on an engine while they were there, and he'd taken it all apart to clean and repair or replace pieces, as needed. As he was putting it back together, they couldn't remember which way the head gaskets went. Dad had never really worked on a car before, but he took one look at it and told them how to fix it. It just made sense to him.

When they returned to O'Donnell for a stretch, Dad and Uncle Leo got a handful of odd jobs to help the family with money. One of the jobs Dad got was cutting the lawn for Dan Blocker's family, who owned the grocery store in town, and Uncle Leo got a job sweeping the floor and cleaning the tables at the local pool hall. They also both worked at the laundromat, and Dad got a job at the town newspaper, where he learned to run a linotype machine and set block text on the printing press. None of the jobs were full-time, so they'd go to one, work for a bit, and then go to the next.

Ysidoro and Cresencia Pisano, my great-grandparents (the ones sitting)

Both Uncle Leo and Dad learned to drive while in O'Donnell behind the wheel of Sammy's car. It had a manual transmission. Dad couldn't remember what kind of car that was, but he remembered driving Sammy's '59 Ford convertible when they moved back to Greeley. The Ford had a hard top that folded into the trunk. They also had a '54 Mercury that my grandma drove. There was another car that they kept on Great Grandpa Pisano's farm. Maybe they were fixing it up or something, because somewhere along the line Dad fell in love with fixing up cars. As far back as I can remember, he had a car at our house he was repairing to resell.

Sammy was a good stepdad to the two of them, though he was maybe a little crazy at times. One time Sammy and Leo were messing around with BB guns, shooting at each other, and Leo shot out one of Sammy's teeth! I can only imagine how crazy that must've been. I wonder who Grandma Mary was more upset with: Leo or Sammy?

O'Donnell wasn't very big. On the main street, there was Blocker's grocery store, the laundromat, and the newspaper office that printed a four-page daily. There was also a restaurant and a movie theater, which were across the street from the roller-skating rink. The pool hall, where Uncle Leo worked, was just around the corner from the restaurant and movie theater.

Dad and Uncle Leo didn't play pool again after Grandpa Manuel died until they moved to

O'Donnell. They would go and play together before Uncle Leo had to clean up the pool hall for the night. The hall had a couple nine-foot tables and two ten-foot snooker tables. Games were five or ten cents a rack, depending on what kind of table you played on. You didn't put your money into the tables like you do today, but the guy who ran the place would come over and rack the balls for you; then he'd collect the money. Dad said they had a custom that if anyone ran the last six balls of a snooker rack, the owner would buy a round of Cokes for the house.

Dad had fond memories of playing in O'Donnell. I think that's where he learned to love the game for himself. I know it must've made him and Leo feel like their dad was back with them again, playing at another table nearby. The pool hall was always a second home to Dad.

He once told me that Uncle Leo was always a better player than he was back in those days. He didn't remember ever beating him. Once they were on their own, it wasn't long before Uncle Leo started playing for money. Uncle Leo was about sixteen, and Dad would have been fifteen. Leo rarely lost. His taste for winning pushed him to keep practicing and getting better. As the little brother, Dad was always trying to catch up.

Leo got so good that if he came in without any money to wager, Dad or another friend would back him, and then Leo would share part of the winnings. Leo was careful whom he'd agree to play, so he almost always won. Every dime counted in those days, so it felt good to win. It was nice to have a few dollars to give their mother when they got home. It also felt good to be better than most of the grown men who came to play.

In the end, though, Leo didn't like Texas much and decided to return to Colorado. When Sammy and his mom said they didn't want to move, Uncle Leo set off on his own and hitchhiked all the way back to Greeley, where he went to stay with Grandpa Pisano on his farm. Sometime in 1965, the rest of the family followed him and settled in Greeley.

A Solid Foundation

Dad used to always tell me that a good pool shot begins with your stance—a solid foundation. He said that a good pool stance is the foundation of a good shooter. Even if the shot is perfectly lined up with the pocket, if your stance is off, your shot will be off. He said that if your base isn't right but you still make the shot, then you are making an adjustment without realizing it, which will reduce your overall consistency. This means you're getting lucky now and then rather than aiming correctly. If your stance is off, your aim-line will always be slightly off. The tougher the shot and the tighter the pocket, the more you're likely to miss when your fundamental foundation is off.

He said he knew players who had shot with a bad base for years without realizing it. By compensating without realizing it, these players will never really know what was untrue about a shot that misses. They've added unnecessary variables to the process, so they never really know which one caused the miss, why the cue ball ended up in the wrong place, or if there is some quirk in the table. Lack of a solid foundation will result in a lack of growth because you're always guessing at why you missed and what you need to correct.

Dad emphasized that the key to a good stance is to line up your body and pool cue with the aim-line. The aim-line is the line, or path, that you want the cue ball to follow after contacting the tip of your pool cue. He said that the middle of your back foot (right foot if you're a right-handed player, for example) should be in line with the path that you want the cue ball to take. Your back foot should be angled slightly outward to keep it comfortably on the aim-line as you set your front foot in place. Once your back foot is in place, take your front foot and step toward the table at an angle so that you feel solid and comfortable on the shot.

After learning and practicing a comfortable stance, my dad taught me how to hold the pool cue. He said it was important for your cue-holding hand to find a place on the back, or butt, of the pool cue, along the wrap, that feels the most comfortable, somewhere close to the balance point. Ideally, if your arm is pointing down at the point of contact with the cue ball, then you're holding it in the right place. Dad always said it was important to have a loose grip on the pool cue, like how you would hold a baby's hand. Holding the pool cue too tightly will make it difficult to have good follow-through on your stroke.

Your left arm (for right-handed players) is your non-cue-holding hand and should be on the table, holding the front, or shaft, of the pool cue parallel with the floor. The way you hold the shaft of the pool cue with your non-cue-holding hand is called a bridge. Dad said that a good bridge needs to have a solid foundation and allow the shaft of the pool cue to move smoothly through it. He taught me different types of bridge options but said that I should find a bridge that is best and most comfortable for me and the shot I was facing.

The open bridge was the easiest bridge to learn. It's easy to set up, gives a solid foundation, and allows for the most visibility when stroking the cue ball. To create a basic open bridge, press your thumb against your pointer finger to make a V groove for the shaft of your pool cue to rest on, and then place your palm and remaining fingers on the pool table. Make sure that your palm and fingers are planted to give yourself a stable pool bridge that won't move as you hit the ball.

Another option he showed me was the closed bridge. To make a closed bridge, make a loop around the shaft of the pool cue with your pointer finger and squeeze it against your thumb. Make sure not to squeeze too tightly to give the shaft of the pool cue room to move comfortably through your bridge. Use your palm and your other three fingers for stability on the table, and that should complete your closed bridge.

Dad then began to teach me the mechanics of the stroke. He said that the best stroke comes from your cue-holding arm moving back and forth like a pendulum, commonly known as the pendulum stroke.

For a pendulum stroke, your cue-holding arm (right arm for right-handed players) should move back and forth like a pendulum during your practice strokes and upon contacting the cue ball. Nothing but your elbow and the lower part of your arm should be moving during the stroke. The rest of your body should be still. Upon contacting the cue ball with your pool cue, he said it is extremely important to follow through and stay down during and for a few seconds after the shot. He said that when you follow through, the tip of your pool cue should go all the way through the cue ball. Your follow-through is what puts spin, or English, on the cue ball (which we'll talk about in a later chapter). The pool cue should be literally pushing the cue ball upon contact with acceleration. The acceleration *through* the cue ball is what puts English on the ball, not the speed or how hard you hit the cue ball.

One thing a lot of beginning players do is hit the ball hard and then pop up as soon as they strike the cue ball. I certainly did when I first started. This can cause all kinds of errors and makes it hard to hit the cue ball consistently in the spot you want because too often you're popping up in the midst of striking the ball, causing the tip of your pool cue to hit the cue ball in a different spot than where you were aiming.

I remember my dad cautioning me when I first started playing to "hit through" the ball and stay down until the cue ball made contact with the object ball. I always wanted to jump up and get right on to the next shot. Instead, my dad always emphasized being patient, staying down, and following through with my stroke.

He always taught you should stay down and hit through the ball with finesse, adjusting the power you use depending on how far you want the cue ball to travel after it hits the object ball. Think of your stroke like a pendulum, he said, swinging back and then forward at the same pace from your elbow—not jerky—and striking through the ball, staying down until the cue ball contacts the object ball or comes to a rest. Your elbow should stay in the same place at the top of the pendulum from the backstroke all the way until the follow-through. The grip of your back hand should be loose, and your wrist should be firm but not rigid, moving just a little to keep your pool cue as level to the table as possible with a slight drop toward the table at the very end. Your cue-holding hand should come up a bit toward your face rather than sliding left or right. If your grip is too tight, you tend to veer to the side rather than hitting straight through, "steering" the ball, creating spin you neither want nor can control. Keep your head up and your body comfortably spaced away from the pool cue to keep it from hitting your body and changing its angle. The tip of your pool cue should follow the ball in the direction of your shot for as far as possible. I can still hear my dad saying, "Stay down and follow through. Get the fundamentals down, and then you can grow from there."

A lot of beginning players are too impatient to practice these fundamentals—they want to get right into shooting balls. Instead, each time they play, they should first practice shooting the cue ball straight down the table and back again on the same line, and then do it from a couple of different places on the table, checking their stance and being sure to follow through and stay down until the ball hits the end rail and rolls straight back to the tip of their pool cue. If it doesn't come back straight, you're not hitting it square enough. Do that for a while and then you can learn how to play, because then you'll know that you're accurately sending the cue ball where you want. This will allow you to grow as a player, because the reaction of the cue ball doesn't lie. You'll be able to see and learn from how the cue ball is interacting with the other balls.

Dad competing in Las Vegas

This is also the place from which you can begin to play with English by contacting the cue ball in different places for different results, getting the object ball to do what you want it to do and controlling the cue ball to line up your next shot. This means everything from getting the cue ball to stop upon contact on a straight-in shot or trying a massé shot around another ball. None of this is possible until you learn to hit the center of the ball with a consistent pendulum stroke each time.

Once you learn these fundamentals, then you can start to do things with the cue ball that are pretty darn fun and cool. You get to expand and try new things. That's when the fun really comes in, because your game evolves—you start being able to get creative and see where your skills will take you.

And that is where getting good at the game really begins.

Are You Standing on Solid Ground?

In their book, *The Faith Code*, Pastor Terry Brisbane and entrepreneur Rusty Rueff repeatedly refer to a saying by Archimedes, the famous Greek mathematician and inventor: "Give me a lever and a place to stand, and I will move the earth."[7] Why? Because this makes you ask a couple of simple but important questions:

1. What is your lever? (Why are you here? What's your purpose?)
2. What are you standing on? (What is the foundation upon which you are building your life?) Is it solid ground?
3. And how are you using these to influence the world around you?

All of us want to live a life worth living, but it's incredibly easy to get sucked along in the currents created by others and miss out on what it really means to live a good life. Pleasures—like the thrill of winning a game of pool—are fleeting. Many who chase only that tend to end up, later in life, questioning where things went wrong. This tends to be because they don't really have a place to stand—something solid they are basing their lives on—or something to stand for that positively impacts others.

It reminds me of a time when there was a tournament in Casper, Wyoming. A bunch of guys from Wyoming had seen Dad play in Greeley and wanted him to come play in their tournament. As I said before, he always drew a bit of a crowd, and he was well-known in the pool world, even in the surrounding states. If he was participating in a tournament, some people would come just to see him again and catch up. He was always a draw.

The problem was that they held the tournament in a stock show building with concrete floors. The concrete floors were slick, and it was sometimes hard for my dad to get the best footing on them because his crutch would slip. He always preferred playing on carpeting or rough-wood flooring.

They wanted him to come so badly, though, they made a deal with him. One of the guys owned a carpet store and said he would donate a carpet to put under one of the tables and they would make sure all of Dad's matches were played on that table. Dad was flattered and agreed to go, and everyone had a great time. He played strong and finished third.

It's obvious to me as I look back that, in a similar way, Dad based his life on ground where he could keep good footing. He'd seen the worst the world had to offer in war, and surviving and thriving after that served to strengthen the faith he'd carried with him from childhood. He always valued family and community first, and then came his fun, which I think he exercised in being an entrepreneur, fixing cars and electronics, and playing pool. He worked hard to support his family and made friends wherever he went. If you ever spoke with him, he was going to help you grow as a human being in some small way, even if it was just to improve your pool game. Really, if I were to sum it up, like Brisbane and Rueff do, I would say he built his life on love—loving God, loving people, and loving what he did, whether it was work or play. His activities were always about what he could give to or do for others. It was also about what he could teach others to do for themselves—how he could make them more competent at doing the important and fun things in life.

In *The Faith Code*, Pastor Brisbane shares a story Jesus told that I have thought of often. Jesus tells the story of two men who both build houses, but one is built on shifting sand and the other on solid rock. Both homes look great, but then a storm comes, and the house built on the sand collapses while the other suffers little to no damage.

As someone who has built a business on repairing work that wasn't done with the proper foundation to begin with (which I'll talk more about later), I know the value of the right base materials to build on in construction. Anything else will look good for a while, but with time and when weathered enough, the quality of the original workmanship will show through. Taking a bit more time to do the work correctly the first time will determine whether the construction lasts years or decades.

Life is best built on things that will stand the tests of time and hardships. No one lives a life without hardships. Spend time building relationships—around both the dinner table and the pool table—and the friends you make will be there to support you for the long run. Faith, family, friends, work, and fun all have a place in building a good life, but you have to keep them in the right order. When my dad came back from Vietnam injured, I know it was the relationships with family—particularly my mom—that helped him not only survive his injuries, but go on to live a fulfilling and purposeful life.

Shooting Straight

A proper base is key to shooting straight in pool, and I have to say, I think the same is true in life. A lot of people think cutting corners is the way to get ahead. They want to save pennies off their expenses or investment and think those things will get them ahead more quickly, but those gains are always short-term. Eventually you'll get a reputation for being cheap or using poor craftsmanship, and that eventually puts you much further behind than if you'd done the work honestly and up-front in the first place. Not only that, but bad reputations are difficult to repair. For every one-star review, you need a dozen or more five-star reviews to compensate.

Because of this, just like your stance in pool, it matters what you're building your life on. Don't skimp on living according to solid values: faith, family, friendship, and craftsmanship in whatever form it takes in the work you do and even in the fun you have. Life isn't worth living halfway. If you can't put your heart into something, it's worth reevaluating whether or not it's worth doing at all. Putting your heart into what is before you to do next is the only way you can free yourself of the baggage of the past and come to each shot—and each relationship and activity—undistracted and ready to give it your best.

THREE

Play the Table

> In pool, your opponent is the least of your concerns. In fact, he or she is a potential friend.
> —Manuel Gonzales Jr.

By the time I was fifteen, I was starting to play in tournaments more often and began doing fairly well. The more I played, the more I saw the same guys over and over again. One of the guys I saw often was named Ben Manzanares. He was one of the top players in northern Colorado. After he beat me a couple of times, every time I saw his name in the draws, I started getting nervous. If he was in the tournament, I knew at some point we'd have to play. He was intimidating, not only because he was good but also because of the way he carried himself. He was confident. He always acted as if there was no doubt he'd run the table if you made the slightest mistake. It seemed to affect the very air in the room.

I started feeling beat before I even got to the table to play him. It wasn't just me either. I'd watch people play him, and you could see it in their eyes and their body language. You could see they were scared to make a mistake because, if they did, they wouldn't get the table back. And you can't play brave if you're nervous. You have to play to make shots, not play not to miss.

One time, early in a tournament, I saw his name, and I must have made some offhand comment to my dad that let him know I was concerned I might run into Ben in an early round.

"But you're not even playing Ben," my dad said.

"Yeah," I said, "but I will."

"No, you won't," my dad shot back.

I looked at him blankly.

"Even when he's standing across the table from you, you're not playing him."

"What?" I asked. "What do you mean?"

"It doesn't matter who's across the table from you. You're not playing them," he went on. "No matter who you're playing, it's not about them. It's you against the table. It's always about where the balls are, how the rails work, how level each part of the table is. You're never playing other people, and they're never playing you. You're playing the table, no matter what happens or who you're competing with."

I'd never thought of it that way before, but it made sense. It wasn't about the other guy, especially if I didn't miss. No matter what I did, it wasn't the other guy who was going to mess me up; it was the lay of the table and the way I controlled the cue ball. Nothing else mattered.

The game changed for me when my dad told me that. The next time I got to a table, I started paying more attention to how the balls rolled, how the ball settled if I hit a touch shot, how the rails worked, and how tight or forgiving the pockets were. Anytime I started to get nervous, I reminded myself that it was just me and the table. It was almost like I could do that "clear the mechanism" thing from *For the Love of the Game*. It helped me focus at a new level. My dad altogether changed my perception of playing pool.

That's when I began to realize that every pool table is a little different. Even the time of day and temperature in the room can change things slightly. The same table will play a little differently if the humidity is different from the last time you played on it. It didn't matter if all the tables in a tournament were the same brand or how hard officials had worked to make sure they were uniform; every table would play slightly differently. The cloth on the table would be worn differently or have a dirty spot or two that could catch balls; the bounce off different rails would be deader or livelier; how the ball ran on different areas of the slate varied slightly, and even the pockets might play larger or smaller depending on how long the table had been in use. Even the condition of the balls on the table can change a game. Noticing one of these small nuances in the course of a game can make all the difference between running the table and missing a shot and losing the chance to shoot again.

Realizing all this gave me a huge confidence boost. It also simplified the game. The more you understand something, the more confident you can be in addressing it. Knowledge breeds self-assurance. All the different factors that could be brought in by a different player became irrelevant. Everything in the game was suddenly within my control. Before that, I would wonder if I was just starting to play badly when I went to a new table and missed a shot, but now I understood that it was more likely a difference in the table, because I had spent so much time making my stance and shooting consistent. My dad once told a good friend we used to play with a lot, Brian Griego, that he needed to "learn the shot and speed of every table," instead of just hitting the cue ball a hundred miles an hour every time.

Once I knew it was more likely the table, I just had to figure out how to compensate for that difference, and I could win the game. It changed the way I spoke to myself as well. It was no longer, *Oh, you're just playing bad*, but I could problem solve instead. I could dissect each part of a shot to figure out where it went wrong, and when I figured that out, I could also figure out how to fix it.

When I would see other guys miss a shot and get frustrated, then I knew they didn't know this. Instead of adjusting to the table, they would just get down on themselves, and that never helped anyone.

And again, this points back to the fact that the cue ball doesn't lie. In pool there are no "mistakes" per se. It's all physics. You may get the physics wrong, but that doesn't change the physics. The math will be the same every time. Each table has a "true way" to play it that needs to be discovered and won't change over the course of a game unless there's a dramatic change in the room's humidity or something, which I've never seen happen in the course of one game.

So there is a "true way" to play each game in and of itself. There are no mistakes; there is only learning. Pool is not about your deficiencies, but about your adjustments. You should be learning from every shot, and misses usually have more to teach you than shots you make.

I don't exactly remember if it was that tournament or one a little later, but it wasn't long before I beat Ben and went on to win my first state tournament where I was the only teenager playing against older men. "Playing the table" was also something that really helped me when we went to Las Vegas to play in the Valley National 8-Ball League Association(VNEA) International Amateur Team Tournament, which we won a couple of years later. I had never been on a stage like that before, but it didn't faze me. By then I was able to lock in on playing the table and shut everything else out.

Since then, I think it's one of the best pieces of advice I can share with other players, and I do all the time—and like Dad's other advice, it doesn't just apply to pool. I think he learned it growing up.

Teen Years in Greeley

Once their family relocated to Greeley, Dad and Uncle Leo slowly began playing all over the area. They played regularly in a couple of places in Greeley. Back then it was Stockman's (owned by Marcelino Stockman—then it became Dutch's, owned by Dutch Klinginsmith), Sportsman's (which was across the street from the old police station), or the Pool Palace (where the owner used to sleep on a couch when things got slow, even if someone was there playing). The Pool Palace had four snooker tables and two nine-foot tables. Most of those places changed owners and names by the time I started playing. Sometimes Dad and Uncle Leo went to Eaton to play, and other times as far as Denver. The pool hall they liked in Eaton had tables, a hamburger joint, and drinks. Dad and Uncle Leo had friends who went to school in Eaton, which wasn't far away, so they would go there for lunch. Sometimes they would stay and skip school to play all through the afternoon.

There was one group that liked to play pea ball at Sportsman's, which is a game where everyone draws two "peas" with a number on them out of a shaker bottle (or the zero pea, which was a free number), then tries to sink their balls before anyone else's, so they could have a shot at the winning eight ball. Players had to work sequentially through the balls either up from the one ball or down from the fifteen. You always had to make contact with the next numbered ball in line, or you could carom off it, if you could figure out how to sink your ball doing so. It allowed up to seven people to play at a time on one table. Everyone would put in a quarter, and the winner would take the pot. My dad played a lot of pea ball because everyone wanted to play with him, so that was easier than playing all of them one by one.

Back in 1966, my dad remembers watching Uncle Leo play a local pro player named Danny Medina. He said Uncle Leo took $800 off him playing nine-ball. There weren't too many around who could beat Uncle Leo at the time. Maybe Gordy Hubert on the snooker table, but Uncle Leo would never play Gordy for money. If money was on the line, Uncle Leo always made sure he had an edge. My dad said that during that time, a well-known pro named Steve "The Miz" Mizerack came through and saw Uncle Leo play. Steve invited my uncle to travel on the road playing pool for money with him, but Uncle Leo didn't want to leave home.

My dad even remembers a time they were playing snooker and Uncle Leo broke, making a ball, and then he ran the table after that. Besides Gordy, he'd never seen anyone do that before. Snooker is considered the real pool players' game. Beginners play pea-ball or eight-ball, more experienced guys play nine-ball, and the best players play snooker.

If any of their friends were going to go play pool, they made sure my dad and Leo would be there too. A favorite place was a bar on Ninth Avenue, across the street from a junkyard, that had two tables. If a new guy came in and Uncle Leo wasn't there, the regulars would set the guy up to play Uncle Leo when he came in. If it turned out well, Uncle Leo would give them a few bucks from the pot when he won.

When he was seventeen, Uncle Leo got a serious girlfriend and pretty much stopped playing cold turkey. Dad always thought that if he hadn't stopped, Leo might have been one of the best players ever—at least in Colorado, for sure.

My sister Renee and Dad's '55 Chevy

Those were the years Dad found his love of working on cars as well. I think my dad remembered every car he ever worked on. Before he left for Vietnam, he had a '49 Mercury, a '57 Chevy, and a '64 Impala he was fixing up all at the same time. He'd drive whichever one had its engine together and was running at the time. At one point, he bought a green '54 Chevy with no transmission. It was a four-door, but the rear door on the driver's side was smashed in, and it wouldn't open. He bought the car for thirty dollars and installed a transmission he bought for twenty-five dollars. He had a car to drive for under a hundred dollars, which was a really good deal even back in the '60s. The car he had the longest was a '55 Chevy he'd bought for two hundred dollars and fixed up.

When Dad was about sixteen, he dropped out of tenth grade and started working in the fields around Greeley. Sometimes he would work clearing irrigation ditches. Whatever he earned, he gave to his mom to help provide for the family. At that time, he wasn't much for school learning but loved to learn about practical things like fixing or making things. It didn't take him long to figure out field work was hard, and he wanted to get more schooling to learn a trade. When he found out the army would pay for schooling after he got out, he decided to look into joining the military like a lot of his friends were doing, even if it meant going to Vietnam to fight. Things were a little tense at home between his mom and his stepdad, so he also wanted out of the house.

When he went to the recruiter, he learned that if he volunteered to go into the service, it was a for a minimum of three years, but if you got drafted, the commitment was only two. Because they were eager to get more recruits, the recruiter told him he could volunteer to be drafted and only have to serve two years. So he volunteered and joined the service as a draftee. Several of his friends had gotten drafted, so it didn't feel out of place. He was working on a farm laying irrigation pipe when his letter came with instructions for when and where to report to catch his bus for boot camp.

It was a sunny morning in mid-July of 1967 when his bus pulled out of downtown Greeley filled with young men wondering about their futures. It wasn't a happy bunch. Mostly draftees, some were angry, some fidgeted anxiously, and others just stared blankly out the window at the passing farmland, wondering if they would ever see it again. It was not a chatty ride.

The night before, there had been a going-away party, and Dad got to meet several other guys who would be on the bus with him the next morning. A handful of them drank some beer together and agreed to stay in touch and reconnect when they all got back. One of them was Ignacio Ramos, who everyone called Nacho. Nacho took one of the beers and said they would drink it together when they all got back. He kept that beer with him the entire time he was in training and through his time in Vietnam, even though it almost got him in trouble with his CO (commanding officer) at boot camp. His sergeant thought Nacho was sneaking alcohol into the barracks against the rules, but when the CO heard why Nacho had it, he dismissed him without a further word being said.

Another was Larry Whisenhunt, who had long hair down to his shoulders and went to a Yardbirds (which later became Led Zeppelin) concert the night before the bus ride rather than the good-bye party. He got all that hair cut off, of course, the very first day at camp. By the time he got to Vietnam, he didn't give that haircut a second thought.

The bus went first to Denver, where they went through medical exams, and then they boarded an airplane for Fort Campbell, Kentucky. For many of them, it was the first time they had left home, let alone left the state of Colorado. Dad was eighteen and would turn nineteen at the end of the next month.

Success Could Be Only One Step Away

In his book *Where Good Ideas Come From*, Steven Johnson makes the point that what you don't know can hurt you and often does. According to Johnson, the world is full of incomplete ideas looking for their counterparts so they can become whole and useful. He points to the printing press as an example. "As many scholars have noted, Gutenberg's printing press was a classic combination innovation, more bricolage than breakthrough. Each of the key elements that made it such a transformative machine—the moveable type, the ink, the paper, and the press itself—had been developed separately well before Gutenberg printed his first Bible."[8]

Paper and ink had been around for years, of course, and were used widely by scribes to create books by hand. Moveable type was created by a Chinese blacksmith, but the application—hand rubbing the paper to create the characters—wasn't much more efficient than what the scribes were doing. The key was combining those things with a screw press invented in Rhineland for crushing grapes to make wine, though it didn't do a great job of it. The press created tremendous pressure evenly over an area, and the action could be done again and again with little fatigue. Combining the press with a table to hold the type, ink it, place a sheet of paper on it, and pulling a lever to close it and make an impression, allowed for multiple pages to be created over and over again dozens of times faster than a scribe could make a copy. The innovative combination of these three things allowed for the creation of the technology that has had the greatest impact on the progress of humanity—the mass production of books. For the first time in history, knowledge, wisdom, and understanding could be handed down person to person throughout a nation. It made schooling possible and led to the formation of a middle class as well as many other innovations.

A lot of us have half-baked ideas or skills that we often undervalue, but the truth is, they might be extremely valuable in a different context. For me, I had solid skills as a pool player, but I was losing the mental game to players more experienced than I was. With one valuable concept—that I wasn't playing my opponents, but the table itself—I got my head right, and my game followed suit. What I didn't know was hurting me, and when my more experienced dad laid a little wisdom on me, it changed everything.

People tend to walk through life with their heads down, underestimating their gifts and abilities and believing what do-nothings have to say about them. Everyone has natural talent in something. They just need to find the place it fits, which can be a long, confusing journey. For me, I was extremely lucky to have the family I did and a dad who knew how to bring natural talent out of me. I was good at pool and got better very quickly because I had such a great teacher in him. I was also lucky that he inspired me to get better and to do the work necessary to create the skills I needed to win.

In his book, Mr. Johnson points out that when people started living in cities, in close proximity to one another, innovation exploded because it was so much easier for incomplete ideas to find their mates. Needs were also amplified so much that meeting them became valuable, and entrepreneurship was born. The printing press, of course, magnified that further, and education helped people connect even more half-baked ideas into whole inventions that continue to accelerate progress even today.

So keep your head up and stay curious. You never know how the next thing you learn might change your life—or your pool game!

Seeing What Others Overlook

Dad was always on the lookout for opportunities. At one point, at the VNEA International Championships in Las Vegas, back when all the tables took one-dollar Susan B. Anthony coins, the habit was that the two players would put a handful of coins by the coin slot to last their match, however many games that might be. People did this so automatically they would leave their coins there when they were done with their match if it didn't go the full games possible.

One night when all the matches were done, and when he was, once again, the last one there, my dad noticed this and went around to all the tables and collected up all the forgotten coins. He said he could sometimes collect as much as fifty to a hundred dollars a night doing this. If he had his wheelchair with him, he could get around the tables pretty quickly, systematically working them row by row.

He never told anyone he did this because he didn't want anyone else to figure it out. He laughed when he told me. Eventually they changed to tokens when games got more expensive than a dollar, and people started remembering to get them each night. Still, he got some good pocket money doing this.

Dad competing from his wheelchair

He was also resourceful when it came to cars. Because he liked working on cars, he'd buy cars that other people had given up on, haul them to the house, do any body work that needed to be done, and get them running again to resell. If anyone in the family had a car issue, they would bring it to him to fix.

On Saturdays he'd often get an itch to work on another car. My mom would pack a picnic lunch, and we'd pile into the station wagon and start driving around looking for a car that obviously hadn't been moved in a while. If we saw one, we'd stop and he'd start talking with the people whose yard it sat in, negotiate a deal, and then put the car on our trailer to haul it to our house. Sometimes we'd go as far as Kansas to find cars. He seemed to have a nose for where to find them.

At times he'd have as many as five or six cars lined up at the house waiting to get worked on. When he finished one, we'd move it out and the next one in. My mom would help trim the grass and weeds that had grown under the moved car, then move the next car into its spot, and continue, plot of grass by plot of grass.

My mom and dad would also go to garage sales and buy antiques, repair any damage to them, then take them to the auction house to resell. They got quite good at repairing things without leaving any evidence they had been worked on.

There are opportunities all around us, but we don't see them if we don't train our eyes to see them. Dad had that eye and taught all of us kids how to have it too. I've always been grateful for that.

FOUR

Begin with Victory in Mind

> On your first shot, find the winning ball and then create a pattern backward from it for running the table.
> —Manuel Gonzales Jr.

It's a simple principle, but a lot of players don't use it. Let's say you're playing eight-ball. Dad taught me to come to a table after the break for my first shot, look over the table, and find the eight ball. Imagine where the cue ball should be for me to sink the eight easily, and then begin to work backward. He said for me to ask myself, *What shot would I want to make to set up the eight?*

Then keep going.

In doing this, as Dad pointed out, I started to see groups. These three balls are a group I could sink together pretty easily, then these two over here, and so on.

At most, there are seven balls between you and the eight. If the table is still open—in other words, nothing has gone in yet, so you can be either solids or stripes—you want to do this for both options and see whether stripes or solids will give you the best path to running the table. If you pattern them in small groups, it makes it easier to visualize.

This might mean that the first shot you take is not the easiest on the table, but you make a harder shot to get to easier shots down the line. Most people, especially beginners, will just look for the easiest shot and then line up on it, going one by one. That, however, often means having to make a much more difficult shot somewhere along the way to the eight, and that generally results in a miss.

Instead, you should think in threes. You want to sink the ball that sets you up best for the next, and then be in a position for an angle on that ball to set you up to sink the ball after it. It's a thought pattern that takes some time and experience to develop, but eventually it becomes natural.

When I was younger, I was playing a friend of mine named Tony Padilla. Tony broke, and it was just clusters everywhere—no clear shots. He looked at the table and said, "Now, if you can run out on this table, then I'm going to nickname you the Wizard."

As my dad taught me, I looked over the table, found the eight, and worked backward. I knew it would be more difficult than that, because I didn't just have to line up for the next shot; I had to break cluster after cluster apart, and then pattern the table again. I went to work, picking shots where the cue ball would break groups apart, or setting up shots where the cue ball rebounded into clusters to break them up after my ball went in. This cluster over here; then break out this cluster over here. When I sank the eight at the end of my turn, he looked at me and said, "Okay, that's your nickname now. You're the Wizard."

To me, my dad was the wizard; I was just following his advice.

The nickname stuck for a while, but it was really about patterning the balls correctly and making the shot presented once the smoke cleared. I started to notice that most mistakes I made would come from not taking the time to pattern the balls, and that would end up creating tougher shots. Although I got really good at making tough shots, I knew deep down that I never should have allowed them to be that difficult in the first place. If I ended up missing, it was probably because of that, but I kept the nickname because a lot of them I made. Really, though, I needed to take more time patterning the table and controlling the cue better. Truthfully, good players are far more impressed when someone controls the cue ball well than they are when someone makes a great shot.

Nine-ball is harder than eight-ball because the balls have to be made in order, so you have to pattern all of the balls individually rather than in groups. Sometimes you can shorten the journey if you can find a way to make the nine ball after hitting your object ball. (In other words, find a way to ricochet—which is called a carom shot—the nine into a pocket after hitting, for example, the three, since making the nine is what wins you the game.) If an early nine is not an option, then you just keep working the table, keeping an eye on the next consecutive three numbers until you can get a shot on the nine.

At first this will feel like overkill, especially if you miss within a couple of balls and your opponent makes a shot or two that change the layout of the table and you're forced to start all over again. But if you practice doing it each time you approach a table, you'll start seeing patterns without thinking about it. The more you do it, the smaller the game will get. You'll begin to see patterns you've played before. You'll start to see the relationships between the balls differently.

I've never really seen anyone start running tables consistently who didn't look at the game this way. When you do this long enough, clearing the table will become a design in your mind that comes automatically.

I remember watching my dad walk around and around a table at the beginning of a game until a pattern for clearing the table formed. He wouldn't take a shot until it all came together. Then he'd meticulously follow what he had laid out in his mind, shot by shot. It could even look like he wasn't thinking between shots because he already had the order and shots set in his mind.

Boot Camp

Every morning at Fort Campbell started with an early-morning run of five miles or more. Dad said in a lot of ways it felt like all they did was run, like they'd do an entire day of running before breakfast. Nacho was in another platoon—Dad was infantry, and he was artillery—but sometimes they'd see each other passing by in the predawn darkness and give out a shout. That was the only time they ever saw each other, because after that they'd go in different directions.

After breakfast, the day was filled with training to master handling munitions, shooting machine guns, winning hand-to-hand combat, and whatever they needed to learn to be turned into warriors. I believe Dad distinguished himself on the shooting range because of the sharp eye he'd developed shooting pool. They trained all day, with only a little time to themselves in the evening. Many times, they just fell into bed and slept, hoping to catch up on a little sleep before a drill sergeant came bursting into their barracks the next morning to rouse them for another long run.

There was a pool table in the enlisted men's club, though, and every once in a while, Dad would go play. Losing himself in focusing on a shot felt the most like being home Dad could find. He told me on more than one occasion that he considered pool "therapy." And I must say that I wholeheartedly agree.

Dad after training with tear gas

After finishing basic at Fort Campbell, Dad was sent to Fort Polk in Louisiana for more specialized training, then eventually to somewhere in California. Fort Polk was nicknamed "Little Vietnam" because the forests and everglades there were the closest thing in the United States to the jungles of Southeast Asia.

Dad applied for the honor of being the guidon bearer, the man who marched at the front of the troops carrying the flag, or guidon, that bore the regiment's insignia. He was selected from all the others in his platoon. With it came an added level of responsibility. He had to be the first one to every march or activity, or else he could lose the position. On one long march, he remembered getting there early and being told to climb into the jeep where the officers would ride as the soldiers traveled on foot. He obeyed, of course, and was surprised when he ended up riding in the jeep the entire distance while the rest of his platoon marched!

When he got to California, his duties were recut several times, to the point he was accused once of being Absent Without Leave (AWOL) for a week when the army lost track of where he was. He said there wasn't much to do as he waited for duty, so he'd volunteered to work in the laundry. Eventually that got cleared up.

While there, he was promoted to private E-4. Most privates are promoted to an E-2 or E-3 when they ship out, but he was promoted to an E-4 for some reason he never told me. I think it was because of his marksmanship, though, because his service record shows he was recognized as a sharpshooter on the M14 rifle, and his final orders were to man a .50-caliber machine gun in the back of an escort jeep. An E-4 is considered a "specialist," and I think that's why he got an assignment as something more than just a line soldier.

He was already doing what he always did—seeing opportunities and finding a way to excel.

Manuel Gonzales Jr., Private E-4

Begin with the End in Mind

In his bestselling book *The 7 Habits of Highly Effective People*, Stephen Covey uses the same principle for getting things done effectively that my dad taught me for running a table. It is his second principle: begin with the end in mind.

In life and often in business, it's easy to focus on what is easy and convenient rather than what is important. People often focus on getting a job that pays well without thinking too much about whether it's something they will enjoy doing or will give them the kind of life they really want to live. Making more money, for example, can distract away from the fact that you're stepping into a job where you have little control over your time. Rather than focus on the little wins along the way, which can take you in a completely wrong direction, you need to start instead with victory in mind. I can now see how my dad's decision to volunteer to be drafted was part of the path that he saw by looking at what he considered victory: getting trade school paid for upon his return.

Dad was always an entrepreneur, so naturally, when I was young, I decided to start my own business rather than look for a job. When I was nineteen, I started my own stucco company, which, with my dad's help, I ran and grew until 2015. The work was great fun and the money was good, but because of the nature and scale of the business, it demanded that we travel all over for jobs, and I was constantly away from home. We might do a new hotel in Cheyenne one week, and then something in Denver, and then travel and stay in Casper the next week or two. I even went as far as Saginaw, Michigan, one time.

When I was younger, this kind of travel was exciting, but by the early 2010s, I was married with kids, and being away from home all the time started to get draining. For about three years, it felt like a freight train that was moving so fast I couldn't get off it. The money was good, and it would have been easy to focus on that as success. The money allowed us to live in a nice house and go on great vacations, but my kids were growing up without me, and I wanted to be there as they got older. For me, victory began to look different from just having a good bottom line.

I began talking with my wife, Cassandra, about it, and she was supportive. She didn't really like having me gone all the time either. Finally, we got to the point where anything felt better than continuing forward with our present circumstances. She even said it would be better to go broke than never having me around. We needed a change.

The business was charging ahead, though, and there was no easy way just to get off. We had to slow it gradually. I immediately stopped looking for new work, finished up the contracts we had left, and then in 2015, I sold off the business and all its equipment. We sold our house in Greeley and moved to Loveland, just south of Fort Collins. It was time for a new beginning focused on living a fuller kind of life putting family higher on our priority list.

It took about three years from the time we decided to switch gears to when we were actually able to stop working in the business altogether. Once settled in Loveland, I finally had time to focus on being home every night and helping to raise our kids. It was pretty scary not going to work every morning and earning an income, but having faith in the Lord, we knew it was the right thing to do. It was only when we began to settle into a better routine that something new appeared. As the saying goes, when a door closes, God opens a window.

After the move, as we walked around different neighborhoods and shopping areas, I began noticing water damage on many houses and buildings from poor stucco, stone, and caulking installation. Such things don't usually show in five or ten years, but after fifteen to twenty years, moisture can seep in through poor seals and rot the wood base. Rot can easily turn to mold, which can be a health hazard. It's not something most people notice, but because I had worked doing stucco for so long and knew the dangers of doing it incorrectly, I began to notice the damage as I walked around town. It was also something I would never have seen had we stayed in the smaller town of Greeley instead of moving into a suburb of Fort Collins.

I'd point it out to Cassandra or the kids. The more I saw it, the more I realized God was showing me our new business—He was opening that window. I began to see that as much as 80 percent of the installations done over the last twenty years had been done incorrectly and needed to be repaired. Everywhere I looked, I saw signs of rotting wood and water damage that needed to be fixed—things that people with an untrained eye would just think were simply dark spots or stains.

Because I had worked with stucco installation all those years, I already had the expertise to fix this kind of damage and do it right so that it would last decades rather than mere years longer. And there was certainly enough of it to build a business around. It was also something that the community needed. With proper quality control and customer service, which I was also already good at because Dad had trained me in it so well growing up as part of our video rental shop (more on that later), I knew I could turn repairing these buildings into a solid business.

Starting with the end in mind—what "victory" would look like for customers—Cassandra and I started to think about the branding. What people needed was a "doctor" for their injured structures, so we started playing with that, finally settling on Stucco, Stone, and Caulking Doctors—or SSC Doctors, for short. There was no doubt in us that it was inspiration from God.

Being in the repair and reconstruction business, we would position ourselves to diagnose structural "illnesses" and do the "proper surgery" to "restore them to full health." We would be prolongers of life and provide solutions that could affect generations of homeowners and businesspeople. We knew if the work was done right and we kept integrity a priority, word of mouth would lead to more and more referrals, and the business would start growing on its own. We focused solely on remediating water damage issues and reinstalling stucco, stone, and caulking correctly with proper moisture seals. This would help buildings last for decades to come.

In my previous stucco company, we were always chasing contracts with new structures, which could be anywhere within a five-state area. Not only that, but we were constantly bidding against other companies doing similar work, and profit margins could get sliced pretty thin. Advertising was difficult as well because it was hard to know how to get in front of potential clients other than just splashing our name everywhere.

For SSC Doctors, advertising was easier, because all we had to do was show people the problem and let them know we knew how to fix it. I would show people the cracks in the stucco or stone, point out the stains, and encourage them to get it looked at and fixed before they had a major problem and the repair work would get really expensive. I mean, it's much easier to have the caulking redone than have to cut into a wall, fix the wood rot, and then reinstall whatever was over it. Us doing community service-type videos showing people what to look for was far better than people finding out too late, pulling stucco off around a spigot or electrical box that wasn't sealed properly, and seeing a damaged substructure or mold that needed to be addressed. It feels good when you can fix something like that for people. And most of the time they're very grateful.

This also moved us into a world where the competition would be a good deal less. The need for our work would be self-evident once we pointed it out to customers, and our ability to point it out would be its own proof of our expertise. Our work would practically sell itself. At the same time, very rarely would we be bidding against anyone else to do the work instead of negotiating directly with clients. There would also be little need to travel outside of the Fort Collins area. There was plenty of work within an hour's drive. I could work every day and be home every night.

As I heard the founding executive editor of *Wired* magazine, Kevin Kelly, once say, "Don't be the best. Be the only." As it turned out, I was getting out of a glutted market to be all by myself. It created an opportunity for amazing impact.

So in 2016, Cassandra and I opened our new company. For the first two years, I did all the work alone, but now we're growing. (If you ever need to know, I can show you how to set up three stories of scaffolding all by yourself!) When I spoke with potential new clients, my knowledge and experience would shine through, and even though I was technically playing salesman, their need and our reputation did the selling for me. We quickly racked up five-star reviews. Building the business played out just like we had envisioned it.

Sometimes there are misunderstandings or expectations that aren't met or unexpected damage once walls get opened up. Just like you can't shy away from a difficult pool shot, you've got to face these things head-on and make the tough phone call or drive to the unhappy customer's building and see for yourself what's going on. When you see a difficult client is calling, you should answer your phone before the third ring!

Years of watching how my dad dealt with people—both in business and in pool halls—had rubbed off on me, so providing good customer service and knowing how to treat people despite how they treated me became second nature. You run into all kinds of characters playing in pool tournaments, after all, and if you don't know how to handle them with care and respect, they can get into your head and affect your game. You can't avoid people who are difficult. You have to find a way to play even when your opponents are being snarky. You have to meet discomfort head-on, and if you don't have a friendly attitude about it, it can be your downfall. I'd learned that avoiding difficult calls will hurt you in the long run, but if you handle them with grace, they can become your biggest supporters. Every problem solved with a positive and friendly attitude is a win for both you and your client!

Each job I did, I built rapport with the customers just as naturally as I had seen my dad do with other pool players or people who came into his video store. Each job also made me better at each aspect of running the company. I felt like God was always there with me, giving me knowledge, wisdom, and understanding for the task at hand, each step along the way.

It reminds me of the story in the Bible when Peter was out fishing all night and then came in exhausted and disappointed because he hadn't caught a thing. As their boat was pulling up to shore, Jesus told him to cast his net on the other side one last time before they came in. The nets were all stored and ready to be taken ashore, laid out to dry and be mended, but at Jesus's instruction, he got them out, threw them over the side, and netted a catch so large they had trouble bringing it in.

Seeing all the repair work that needed to be done in Loveland and Fort Collins was like throwing a net on the other side of my boat when I thought I was finished. It was the same net I had always used, but doing it this way got new results. It's made all the difference in the world to my family and my enjoyment of life.

The timing was also perfect. If I had tried to do this work when I was younger, the damage wouldn't have been there. If we had stayed in Greeley, I probably never would have seen it. Stucco siding had just started to be popular when I began my first company, and the competition to do it on new homes was intense. Now, over twenty years later, the wear and tear was just starting to show on jobs that hadn't been done well to begin with, and that created a new market for repair work. When God showed me that, I realized it was a unique opportunity.

What I Learned from Pool about Doing Business

Just like what my dad showed me about approaching a pool table after the break, I began my new business by looking at victory and evaluating every other step I would take along the way to creating a business that would support the kind of life I really wanted. In pool, when you do that repeatedly, lining up each shot creates a pattern to systematically work through with plenty of room to adjust if something unexpected happens. In business, I saw similar patterns, according to customer needs, from scheduling to customer care. You've got to be responsive; you've got to do high-quality work; and you've got to handle the business side of things like a pro with proper billing, accounting, and team management. It's not rocket science, but doing it right takes diligence and the willingness to learn from mistakes.

CONTROL THE ROCK

In playing pool, the game constantly changes. Each shot creates a different playing field. Once a ball is off the table, new opportunities arise that you may have anticipated but that didn't really present themselves until the balls settle. What was a *maybe* before becomes a primary goal. Possibilities and priorities have shifted. The table is a new landscape.

Again, we looked at what victory for my family and our new company would look like, and then we backtracked to what we would need to accomplish to get there. Then all we needed to do was line up those things correctly and make our "shots" count. In these things, just as when I approach a table after the break, I could see a path to victory laid out before me.

Not only that, but it's also meant I now have time to be home and practice pool again, which I had all but given up after winning the VNEA Masters Team Championships in 2006. Now I'm thinking again about playing tournaments with my sons, Manuel IV, Carlos, and Isaiah, and a couple of my nephews, Luis and C.J., just like my dad did with me. I can hardly wait.

FIVE

Limitations Aren't Always Limitations

> You can do anything if you put your heart into it.
> —Manuel Gonzales Jr.

My mom's maiden name is Dolores Marie Gomez, but she was christened Guadalupé at her baptism, so she was always known as Lupé to the family and Lulu to her friends. She knew Dad from when they were younger, but said she'd never really spoken with him much, even though she and my Aunt Mary Helen would hang out at the Gonzales family house on Ninth Avenue and Second Street in Greeley. That was where she first met Dad, but she thought he never really noticed her. Still, she thought he was handsome.

Mom's brother Tommy was friends with Uncle Leo as well, and sometimes Dad would come over to the Gomez house at 914 Fourth Street with the two of them. He still never seemed to look her way, or at least that's what she thought. They must've been fifteen or sixteen at the time, not long after the family moved back from Texas.

Soon after Dad had gotten on the bus for Fort Campbell, Kentucky, Mom broke up with the man she was engaged to at the time. He was charming, but he couldn't hold down a steady job because he never wanted to work. Instead, he spent most of his time carousing with his friends and drinking. While Mom wasn't really taken with him, he liked her and was constantly talking about the two of them getting married. She had even begun collecting things they would need for their home—rugs and other household items—once they got married.

One day, though, she saw it would never work. He came over to her friend's house where she had been waiting for him, and he wanted her to come with him to hang out with other friends and drink. She didn't want to, and they got in a fight. Eventually, he left without her. She was so angry, she took all the things she had collected for their house together, went to the other friend's house, threw them at him on the front doorstep, and told him she was done with him.

I think the honest truth, though, was that up to that point Dad just never felt it was the right time to ask her out. After they married, he admitted that one day he saw her walking to school and told a friend, "There goes that little Gomez Girl. I'm going to marry her one of these days."

Apparently, he had noticed her after all.

LIMITATIONS AREN'T ALWAYS LIMITATIONS

Mom and Dad during his leave

Right before he passed away, Dad told Mom he had always loved her and had known he loved her from the first time he saw her. Growing up, though, they were both always dating someone else, so he didn't do anything about it. But it wasn't long after he'd left for boot camp that Dad found out the girlfriend he'd had before leaving was dating other guys. It was a pretty tight Hispanic community in Greeley, and not much didn't get told quickly, so my dad heard about it almost as soon as it happened. He broke up with her as soon as he heard.

My Aunt Pauline with Dad

Since neither he nor my mom were dating anyone else, he knew it was time to do something about it. It was soon after that Mom got a letter from Dad. He said he was coming home for a two-week leave in December, and he wanted to know if she would go out for a Coke with him. She wrote back to tell him yes. They continued to write back and forth after that.

When he came home for leave, the two met to go to a dance at the Good Americans Organization (GAO) in Denver. Every once in a while, the organization had dances and banquets for local Latinos to connect. Dad wore his uniform, and the two of them went with Aunt Pauline (Dad's sister) and Uncle Stevie (Mom's brother), who were friends at the time. For the rest of those two weeks, Mom and Dad dated every night, going roller skating and to other dances or just driving around town in his car and talking. On the last night before he shipped out for Vietnam, Dad proposed, and again, she said yes.

Before Dad left for Vietnam, right before Christmas, he gave my Aunt Pauline his green '54 Chevy, the one with the smashed-in back door (though it was only a dent now that he'd worked on it), since she didn't have a car. He flew to California to await his final orders, and then within a few days, he boarded a plane for Vietnam.

Lining Up Your Shots

I can't remember a time in my life before I had a pool cue in my hand. Dad would take me to the pool halls before I was really old enough to play, and I'd watch him or play pinball the entire time, but we had a snooker table at home. I remember playing there trying to sink balls with my dad as some of my earliest memories. That's where he taught me stance, stroke, aim, everything.

Snooker tables are usually five feet by ten feet—the largest of billiard tables are six feet by twelve feet—and have the tightest pockets. Our snooker table was five feet by ten feet. They're a larger size than standard eight-ball tables. Snooker tables exaggerate the spin you put on the cue ball, and straight shots have to be exact, or each degree off will show by the time the cue ball connects. The tight pockets accentuate accuracy as well. If you're not dead center, the ball will bounce out. It's the most difficult of any table to play on, which makes it the best place to learn.

In a lot of ways, it was that table that taught me how to aim.

Once I developed a routine to my stance, aim-line, and stroke, aiming to make shots that are not straight in was the next big step in getting better at the game. My dad said that although mastering straight-in shots is an essential first step, they are also rare. At least four out of five shots are going to have an angle and require some kind of "cut" to make them. (A "cut shot" is a shot in which the cue ball contacts the object ball off-center to deflect the object ball at an angle.) To be able to make shots with different angles, my dad taught me different aiming techniques. He said it was important to learn different systems to be able to see the shot from different perspectives.

The first aiming system he taught me was to stand in line with the object ball and the pocket I was trying to make it into. From there, I was able to see the "contact point," the exact spot on the object ball that the cue ball would need to hit to send the object ball down the path to the pocket. He then had me keep my focus on that spot as I stood behind the cue ball and began my shot routine. After much practice and learning from misses, I was able to see the path I needed to send the cue ball down, for the correct part of the cue ball to contact the contact point.

Another system my dad taught me was the "ghost ball" aiming system. For this system, the same contact point is used. When lining up the shot, though, Dad would have me imagine the cue ball being right in line with the contact point and the pocket I was trying to make it into. Sometimes while training me, he would physically put another ball in the spot where the cue ball needed to be at the moment of contact with the object ball, so I could get a better visual. Then he'd move the extra ball, and I would shoot the shot imagining the cue ball replacing the ghost ball.

Over time I found that both aiming methods worked great, but of course, they would take practice to perfect. And just as Dad said, because your perception changes on every shot, it's nice to have different aiming methods for different types of shots.

Doing What No One Thought You Could

After he was settled back at home after the war and he began to get better at playing pool again, Dad started going back to some of the places he'd played before the war to get a change of scenery and play against different people. When he went back to the pool hall in Eaton for the first time, the new owner didn't want to let him play. He thought a guy with only one arm and one leg was likely to tear the cloth on the table.

Dad told him, "If I tear the cloth, I'll pay for it. I'll have new cloth put on it and everything." So the guy, still not completely convinced, let him play.

Once Dad started playing, there was instantly a crowd of about half a dozen guys standing around watching him. Seeing what a draw Dad was and how good he was, the owner told him, "You're welcome to come back and play here anytime you want."

Underestimating Dad was a common practice.

When he was back home from the VA hospital, there were certainly things he couldn't do anymore because of his injuries, but Dad wasn't going to accept them without first testing exactly where those limitations were. Honestly, I don't think he really saw limitations as limitations as much as obstacles to overcome—challenges he was going to meet. One time, I came home to find him installing a door that he had somehow carried inside all by himself. He also installed drywall, put in carpeting and tile, and did other construction work, fixing dishwashers and clothes washers and dryers with little to no outside help.

Sometimes Mom would find Dad working on a car and he'd climbed completely inside the engine well getting to a part. My Aunt Pauline said he'd get mad if anyone offered him help before he had tried to do something for himself. He taught himself to do everything from buttoning his shirts and putting on a belt to picking up his crutch if it fell. He even jumped on a trampoline with us when we were growing up.

My Aunt Teresa (Tency), my Aunt Irene (Tiny), a couple of neighbor kids, and the infamous green '53 Chevy

One time my Aunt Pauline needed new brakes on her car, and Dad told her he could change them out. She asked, "Can you do that with one hand?"

He answered, "With your help. I will use my left arm, you sit on a bench in front of me, and you will be my right arm."

She was very pregnant at the time with a big stomach, but she agreed.

She remembers stretching the springs on the brakes as Dad held another part in place. When they were done, she felt like there was nothing she couldn't do. She'd caught a bit of Dad's spirit.

He knew how to cook and loved to bake. When my sisters and I were in elementary school, if there were cupcakes needed for a class party, Dad was the one who made them. We'd sit with him in the kitchen, and he'd give us little jobs to help. With him, everything was a team effort.

Even though he was pretty self-reliant, he wasn't slow to ask for help when he actually needed it. At the same time, I think he often just asked for help so that he could teach something. For instance, he used to have us hold the solder when he needed to solder something inside a VCR he was fixing. He'd carry the VCRs to the worktable himself, though, tucking them between his good arm and his crutch.

He drove his truck by himself. He'd tuck his crutches behind the seat, then jump up inside and drive away. He knew how to get back out and get the crutches himself as well, but if my mom, one of my sisters, or I was with him, we'd grab the crutches and come around to his side of the car so he could take them from us. There are a lot of things those of us with two hands take for granted. Try going a day with one hand always tucked in your pocket, and you can get an idea of it. As far as I know, there wasn't anything he wouldn't first try to do himself.

My sister Renee's husband, Rick, said Dad taught him he could do anything he set his mind to, even though he saw Dad at his weakest. Rick helped him with anything he needed in the last several years of his life, giving him rides to doctor's appointments and fixing things around the house, and he especially treasured his memories of helping Dad work on his '55 Chevy. Even when he could tell things were physically tough for my dad, Rick said he didn't complain and went right on with what he wanted to do that day, just maybe a little more slowly and carefully.

There Are No Mistakes; There Is Only Learning

In her TEDx talk titled "The Power of Yet," Dr. Carol Dweck tells the story of a high school in Chicago where students don't get Fs, but instead the grade is "not yet."[9] In other words, they don't fail classes; they just retake them until they succeed, and then they graduate when they have passed a certain number of courses. As Dr. Dweck put it, "If you get a failing grade, you think, 'I'm nothing; I'm nowhere.' But if you get the grade 'not yet,' you understand that you are on a learning curve. It gives you a path into the future."

In her book *Mindset: The New Psychology of Success*, Dr. Dweck explains that people are sometimes beaten before they even start if they don't carry this "not yet" attitude into daily life. Too many carry what she calls a "fixed mindset" into situations where people determine their self-worth and abilities based on success or failure in a given task at a given time. They tend to overestimate the significance of instances of success or failure rather than look to learn from them. If they fail, they look down on themselves; if they succeed, their sense of accomplishment tends to be overblown. Neither is valuable.

Instead, she encourages having a "growth mindset," meaning that each failure is just a "not there yet" step along the way. The "failure" is always secondary to what is learned through it. Mastery is elusive, and there's no "arrival point" to that journey; there is only constantly getting better. Because of this, it's better to enjoy the journey than to miss living in the moment dreaming about someday "arriving" at a place—like winning a championship or achieving a certain goal—which will be fleeting or merely a stepping-stone to something else.

That's not to say having goals or chasing championships is meaningless, because it is not. What goals and championships should be seen as instead is a challenge to growth, and that growth or improved performance is what should be celebrated, even if it's not a met goal or championship . . . yet.

Watching how my dad addressed challenges while I was growing up gave me confidence in so many ways, especially when he was encouraging me. He certainly knew how to take failures in stride and squeeze learning from them. I could never have started my own company at nineteen without his encouragement, example, and guidance. I remember how scared I was the first time I talked with a client about hiring me and how nervous I was during the installation trying to be sure I did everything right and satisfied the customer.

When I made a mistake, Dad guided me to own up and fix things. I just stuck with it, and the more time I spent taking care of all parts of my business, the better I got at them. A lot of the sales techniques I learned over the years and the customer pointers I know came from him. He had an easy, graceful, and natural way with people that I absorbed while hanging around with him.

If I didn't know how to do something, I learned it with his help, even down to creating my own profit-and-loss statements, finding insurance for workers' comp, or whatever was needed. No matter what it was, he would say, "You can learn how to do it. We can figure it out." Then he'd walk with me as I did.

Pool is definitely a game best played with a growth mindset. Most people I know with fixed mindsets play frustrated most of the time when they meet a better player, or they quit. It takes real determination to practice the same shot over and over again until you get it just right. Shane Van Boening, whom I met in 2006, before he turned pro, and hung out with playing in Las Vegas, spent fifty hours a week practicing—ten hours a day, two or three days a week, just on his break. He has the best break I've ever seen—and quite possibly the best break of all time. He eventually went on to be the top player in the United States. He kept shooting the same shots over and over again, practicing to be the best he could be, and enjoying every day of that journey.

It was that same attitude that helped me become an international champion.

Growing in the Game

After getting pretty good at home on our snooker table, Dad added me as the sixth player on a five-man league team when I was thirteen. We played in the Valley National 8-Ball League Association (VNEA), which is now in thirty states and seven different countries. They sponsor world team competitions every year in Las Vegas. At that time, they didn't have a juniors division. I was one of two players under the age of twenty-one to join a team. The association sponsors both singles and five-man team leagues.

Mostly I played against guys who were much older than I was, but when I was fifteen, my dad entered me into the VNEA Junior National Championships in Missouri, playing in the upper division against mostly eighteen- and nineteen-year-olds. I was just a few days too old to play in the fifteen-and-under division. I did pretty well, finishing in the top sixteen.

Dad's team when I first joined at age thirteen

That same year he entered me into a state tournament in Colorado playing guys in their twenties or older. I started as a C player, the lowest rank, but when I beat the first guy I played four to one, my opponent complained that I was rated too low, so they moved me up to the B rank before the next round. I still won at that level.

Before the tournament, they had what they called a Calcutta auction, where people could bid on players in the tournament they thought would do the best, a little like betting on horses or on the winner of a golf tournament. It's a way for bystanders to get in on the action and raises interest and money for the tournament. Players could go for hundreds of dollars. When I came up, no one bid on this fifteen-year-old kid except my dad. Dad got me for fifteen dollars and ended up winning five hundred when I won the tournament. He couldn't have been prouder.

Dad, the tournament director, me, and Mom when I won the tournament at fifteen

I got to see how well-known my dad was again at that tournament because the guy who won the AAA division, the highest division before pro, came over and talked to him and asked if I was his son. His name was Mike Hellmer. He was probably one of the top three players in Colorado at the time, and I loved to watch him play. I remember pretending to be him when I was younger practicing at home. I'd play as him against Dave Gomez, another of my favorites and a top player, and go back and forth shooting each side of a game.

Eventually, I was fortunate enough to play with Mike in 2006 on a team we took to Las Vegas to play in the master's division of the VNEA International Team Tournament Championships when I was twenty-eight. We took first place.

By the time I was nineteen, I had grown enough to be the best player on Dad's team. Two of northern Colorado's top players, Tony Piazza and Steve Asherin, came to my dad and asked if I could play with them and another strong player, Eric Baumgardner, in the upcoming VNEA International Team Tournament Championships. He didn't hesitate. "You should ask him," he told them. When they asked me and my best friend, James Hilzer, to join the team, I was shocked but conflicted. I was already committed to Dad's team.

Unsure, I asked my dad about it, and he only said, "That's who you should be playing with if you want to get better." I went from being the best player on our team to somewhere in the middle of the pack on this new team. Once again, Dad was right, though. Playing for this new team motivated me to practice even more. Still, I was in awe of how selfless he was and how he wanted what was best for me.

We traveled to Las Vegas to play in the VNEA International Team Championships. There were over five hundred teams in that tournament from all over the world. Because my dad had taken me with him in previous years, I already knew some guys from other teams. Spain had a good team and a guy close to my age named Francisco, whom I had become good friends with. When I went to check out the bracket, he was there.

"Hey, Manuel, how are you doing?"

We chatted a bit, and then he started razzing me: "We've got a good team this year. I think we're going to win it all."

I looked at him and said, "Yeah? Well, you might get second, 'cause we're going to win it." We were just joking back and forth, but as things would have it, we ended up playing each other in the finals.

In a team tournament, each team picks five guys for each round, and each player plays everyone on the other team once, so there are twenty-five games in all. Each game is scored. The winner gets ten points, the loser gets however many balls they sank. So, if you ran a table, the score would be 10–0, but if it came down to the eight ball, it would be 10–7. A running total would be kept, and then once there weren't enough points left for one of the teams to regain the lead, the match would be over.

There's a good bit of strategy that goes into your lineup, because you don't want to end up with your weakest guy playing their best in the last game, but you also need to get to the last game, so it can be bad to "save" your best players who may never play if the other team scores too many points first.

LIMITATIONS AREN'T ALWAYS LIMITATIONS

We had to beat Spain twice in a row in the final because it was a double-elimination tournament, and we came in with one loss. We were definitely the underdogs. Spain's government had put their team together and paid for their players to play (like a lot of teams used to do in the Olympics). A couple of them were in fact pros, but they "snuck in" to this amateur tournament. The most notable players on Spain's team were two-time winner of the World Pool Masters, David Alcaide, and one of Spain's best, Richard Lacey.

In the first match against them, the twenty-fifth and deciding game came down to mine—whoever won it would win the round. My opponent made a few balls and then went for a bank shot, and it came up short, leaving me the table. I cleared the rest of the balls, and he never got another shot. (They ended up sitting him for the final round against us.) I was wearing a John Elway jersey, and I remember the announcer made some comment about me moving through the balls like John Elway works through a defense.

That felt great!

It was really fun. It was up in a penthouse of the casino. There was a crowd and people were chanting, "U-S-A! U-S-A!" I vividly remember the look on my dad's face when I sank the eight. I heard him scream, "That's my boy!"

Now we had to play Spain one more match; the winner would be the champions. With six games left, we were trailing by thirty-six points, so all they needed was twenty-five points to beat us. We managed to get enough points so that by the twenty-fifth game, there was a two-point difference, meaning, again, whoever won that twenty-fifth and deciding game would win the tournament.

The room was tense with everyone's attention on this final break. I remember thinking, *Please make a ball.* When our best player, Tony Piazza, broke, the balls opened up wide and one went in. You could just see the guys on the Spanish team deflate. He ended up running the table, and we won the whole thing. People from all over were celebrating with us and even asking us for our pictures and asking for autographs on their little paper American flags.

That same year, I ended up fifth place in the eight-ball singles, losing to Richard Lacey, and in the top sixteen of the nine-ball singles. I was recognized for high finishes in multiple events and named to the tournament all-star team.

That was the best experience of my pool career by far, and I know I never would have gotten there without my dad's teaching and without mimicking his "play the table" attitude. He later told me that watching us win that international team tournament was the most exciting moment he had experienced in pool. I am still so proud to have been part of it.

SIX

Tinker with Intent

No, I don't know how, but we can figure it out together.
—Manuel Gonzales Jr.

Dad arrived at the Tan Son Nhut Air Base outside Saigon two days before Christmas 1967. Tan Son Nhut was a large US military airfield together with the civilian airport for Saigon and the headquarters of the Republic of Vietnam Air Force. His first post was at Củ Chi Base Camp, headquarters of the Twenty-Fifth Infantry (made famous by the movie *Platoon*), about fifteen miles north of Saigon proper. Bob Hope's USO tour performed there on Christmas Day.

Being a "grunt"—meaning newly arrived—Dad was immediately assigned to guard duty in a foxhole on the perimeter of the base. There were usually two guys at each post for this, but they dropped down to one the day the USO troupe performed. The show featured actress Raquel Welch, singer and actress Barbara McNair, Broadway star Elaine Dunn, reigning Miss World Madeline Hartog-Bel, singer Phil Crosby (one of Bing Crosby's four sons), comedian Earl Wilson, and Les Brown and His Band of Renown. (You can watch footage of the troupe's entire tour on YouTube.) Since he was on guard duty that day, my dad didn't get to see the show.

Once again, his orders were recut because there wasn't a position with an escort unit open for him, and he waited a few more days before being assigned to a mechanical unit as a soldier attached to an M113 armored cavalry assault vehicle, also called an ACAV. These vehicles, the most widely used vehicle of the Vietnam War, actually had several nicknames, including an APC for "armored personnel carrier" or a "1-1-3." Dad's unit called them "tracks" because they had a track like a tank, but without the turreted cannon up top. Tracks were used like a light tank to break through heavy jungle thickets to attack and overrun enemy positions.

Dad was still at Củ Chi over a month later, when, on January 30, 1968, the Viet Cong and the People's Army of Vietnam (PAVN) mounted a major offensive on eight South Vietnamese and American command and control centers in major cities throughout South Vietnam. It was the first attacks of what became known as the Tet Offensive because it took place on the Tet Mau Than holiday, a celebration that marked the beginning of the lunar new year. The next day, on January 31, they would attack 105 more locations.

Dad while on patrol

On guard duty

Among those was the Tan Son Nhut Air Base. About 3:20 a.m. on the thirty-first, tracer rounds were fired toward the fuel depot in the northeastern corner of the airfield; then mortar fire began about ten minutes later on the western extreme to take out the concertina wire and perimeter fences to make a pathway through which ground troops could pass. "When the base perimeter had originally been breached," according to Wikipedia,

> Lieutenant Colonel Jack Garred, the senior advisor to the South Vietnamese Tan Son Nhut Security Forces, requested a U.S. Army Brigade to secure the western flank of the base. II Field Force, Vietnam ordered the 25th Infantry Division at Củ Chi Base Camp, 24 km north of Tan Son Nhut, to send an armored cavalry troop to Hóc Môn District to cut off the anticipated VC route of withdrawal from Tan Son Nhut. At 04:15, the mission was assigned to Lieutenant Colonel Glenn K. Otis's 3rd Squadron, 4th Cavalry Regiment. Otis assigned the mission to his only available forces at Củ Chi, two platoons of Troop C commanded by Captain Leo Virant with a strength of three M48 tanks and ten M113 Armored Cavalry Assault Vehicles (ACAVs). As Troop C left their base at 05:03, the mission was changed from securing Hóc

Môn to counterattacking the VC at Tan Son Nhut.[10]

Track firing a .50 caliber machine gun

Dad was on one of those ten ACAVs. Dad's track was sent to the east side and saw no action, but the ones sent to the west side did. They lost a tank and four M113s, and the soldiers aboard them were either killed or wounded. The fighting went on for a few days before the Viet Cong were pushed completely back. American troops lost 22 soldiers and had 82 injured, the South Vietnamese lost 29 and had 15 injured, while the Viet Cong and the People's Army of Vietnam forces saw 669 killed and 26 captured. The Viet Cong lost most of the battles of this offensive, but it was the beginning of them winning the war. Watching at home, the American public didn't have a stomach for the violence—who would?—and the political will of the people soon turned against it.

Not long after, Dad's track was assigned to escort a convoy from Saigon to Cambodia. In the trip there, nothing happened, but on the way back, the convoy was ambushed, and they lost some friends he had just met. It was a devastating experience and the first time he realized he was really in a war. When I asked him about this battle, he choked up and couldn't talk anymore. I can't imagine what it must be like to remember such things, let alone experience them in the first place.

Track crews stuck together for the most part, and after some time being on the track with the others, Dad's natural mechanical curiosity came to the surface. He'd watch the mechanics work on the track and learned from them. Eventually the driver of Dad's track taught him how to drive it.

Some weeks later, probably early March or late February, Dad was assigned to driving his own track. Because he was now the driver, he got to nickname his vehicle, and it became known as Lulu, after my mom. They painted that name on the side of the vehicle.

At one point, Dad's team got a new track, and they had to move all of their equipment from their old track to a new one. At that point Dad and his gunner took the initiative to organize everything on their new M113 so that they would have quick access to it when needed, be it ammunition, flares, the med kit, or whatever. This wasn't something drivers were trained to do; he came up with the idea on his own.

Dad and "Lulu"

In the middle of doing this organizing, he heard his name called. He turned to see it was his stepdad, Sammy, who had joined the service after he left. They ended up going to the NCO club, getting some beers, catching up, and playing pool until 10:00 p.m., when the club closed.

Soon after that, Dad's platoon was sent out into the field and joined with some other tracks and their soldiers. One of the guys Dad became friends with was Don Fuller, driver of a track nicknamed Lucky 13. Another friend was Myron Peterson, who was part of Don's track crew. Everyone called him "Pete."

Tracks were the center of a group of five or six soldiers: a driver, a gunner, and three or four guys who walked alongside with machine guns. The tracks traveled in groups of four or five. Most of their missions were search and destroy, and they were constantly on the move.

Their units patrolled in the field and went from mission to mission—whatever was radioed in that day. They were in constant communication with artillery that was centrally located behind them, and if they got into a firefight, they could call the artillery units to shell wherever they thought the enemy was hiding, usually in the perimeter of a stand of trees or a ravine. Dad knew Nacho was part of one of these artillery units and sometimes wondered if he was there helping them, loading big shells into those guns firing from miles away.

"Let's Figure It Out Together"

Just like how he organized his track, Dad had a sixth sense about how things went together. It was as if he could see how something worked in his mind's eye and intuitively knew what each part did and where it should fit.

Just a few years before Dad passed away, my sister Denise's husband, Jesse, was trying to fix a dishwasher, and my dad came over. When he asked Dad if he knew how to fix dishwashers, he said, like he always did, "No, but we can figure it out together." It was a mix of understanding how things worked, confidence that he would be able to figure it out, and a refusal to let anyone with a problem face it alone.

I've always had the belief that one of the ways God manifests in our lives is through knowledge, wisdom, and understanding. Knowledge is information about something, wisdom is the insight to practically apply that knowledge, and understanding is a sense of how all the pieces of something go together to make it work, whether that be a dishwasher, balls colliding in sequence on a table, or doing a job correctly so the work will last a long time or function properly. It's something that allows you to see patterns, processes, or strategies—like how to run a table—with your mind's eye. That takes patience as well because the pattern isn't always available right off. Sometimes you have to pace around the table, taking in different angles and getting different perspectives; the pattern is there if you will take time to look for it and have the determination to see it. In this way, I saw my dad walk with God all the time.

He replaced anything he had lost in the war with a dogged determination to figure things out and fix them with the resources he had on hand. It didn't matter what it was. It could be a car engine or a dishwasher or a dryer or a remote-control car. He saw the ways they were similar and the nuances that made them unique. Once you build a basic understanding, you can learn more and more on top of that.

The first time he opened up a VCR when someone brought one into his video store, he had no idea how it worked, though he did have a basic mechanical understanding from other things he had worked on. There was no YouTube at the time to show him what to do. He didn't even have the owner's manual to look at. If you've ever tried to fix something for the first time, you know how quickly it can get frustrating, and you'll want to quit. It's always easier to take a broken thing to someone else and pay them to repair it. Like a true entrepreneur, Dad would take other people's frustrations and turn them into a business. He went from repairing his first VCR to having dozens at a time sitting in his workshop as he worked through them one by one figuring out what was wrong with them. If something really stumped him, he'd make friends with someone who knew more and learn from them. There was a guy in Denver who worked on VCRs whom he would go to with really sticky problems.

I remember going down to Denver with my dad to meet this guy. He'd bring in a couple VCRs and then have the guy walk him through fixing each of them. I know a lot of technicians wouldn't have the patience to do that, but somehow Dad had a way of talking with them and convincing them to teach him rather than just doing it themselves. Dad wouldn't let the guy touch the machines but instead had him watch what he was doing so that Dad did all the work, and then he'd compensate him for his time. Dad was always a great bargainer, and if there was a way to barter rather than pay cash, he'd figure it out. I think he also had a sense that he'd rather trade favors than just have something be transactional. It was more personal that way.

Later in life, he figured out how to fix other electronics, like TVs and even Xboxes. My nephew Vinnie remembers working on those together with him and watching him work the problem each one presented to him. If Dad wanted to do something, he'd figure out a way. Vinnie remembered that he was always tinkering with something, and if he ever called Vinnie to do it with him, Vinnie would always be there if he could.

Learning is huge, and wanting to learn and understand something is powerful. You should always love learning—always want to grow—and that will make you love teaching as well, because you learn things even better when you teach them to someone else. I've always loved learning, and I know I got that from my dad.

My wife and kids say the same thing, and all had their own favorite memories of my dad. My son Manuel VI once remarked that everybody knew if you had anything that was broken, all you had to do was take it to Grandpa, and he would figure out how to fix it. He always gave everything 110 percent. He always did whatever it took to help others.

My daughter Cinnamon remembers he always had a lot of movies and was always excited to show them the newest he had for them to watch. One time when they were watching the movie *Slither*, which is about giant alien worms, my dad came up from behind the couch to scare them, pretending his half arm was a slither. She jumped and then laughed so hard she was in tears.

My daughter Jasmine shared that her grandfather was constantly reminding his grandkids to mind their grandma. He was always looking out for her, but I think, even more, she was always looking out for him. She remembered how happy he always was when he grabbed his cue case and zipped up his jacket as he was going to play league.

My daughter Mariah remembers when she was six and we had a family Halloween party. We had a costume contest, and my dad dressed up as a vampire. Mariah thought he had the best costume, and then he won the prize for best costume! He was also the funniest vampire she had ever seen!

My daughter Selena remembers him giving them each a ride around in his wheelchair with him. She always thought they were going super-fast, though in reality he was really careful with them and just pretending they were going out-of-control fast. When he got a new mechanical arm one time, she thought it was so funny and scary at the same time. It looked so real to her.

My son Rey remembers how kind he was to him every time they were together. They always had fun together.

My son Carlos remembers the rides in his grandpa's wheelchair as well. At one point, Dad got all his grandkids PSP gaming units and new games he'd picked out for each of them, and Carlos remembers how he'd always let the kids "rent" the newest movies in the store for free.

My son Isaiah also remembers taking wheelchair rides and watching movies from the video store his grandpa ran. He also loved watching him build stuff. He remembers thinking how amazing and creative his grandpa was for being able to do everything with only one hand.

My wife, Cassandra, remembers him making fun of her high heels when she'd carry Carlos and Isaiah out to the car in car seats after we'd all been out to a restaurant together. He'd say something like, "I'm not sure those are the best shoes for the task at hand." But she also remembered that, even when giving serious advice, he was never serious. He'd always find a joke to lighten things up.

I'm pretty sure my dad always thought that if we weren't laughing at some point, we weren't having fun, even if we were in the middle of a scary movie or a serious discussion. He used to always use humor to make each kid feel special as well. It was a real talent!

The Stun Shot

Dad said that the most important shot in pool to learn is the "stun shot." The stun is when you hit a cue ball just below center, causing it to slide toward your object ball because there will not be any top or bottom spin. As the slide wears off, the cue ball will start to roll forward, so shots with a longer distance require more speed or a touch lower hit on the cue ball so that the cue ball holds the slide all the way to making contact with the object ball.

Stun is probably the most difficult shot to learn because it's sensitive to how low and how hard you hit the cue ball. It takes a lot of experimenting with it before you really feel like you have control over it.

Using stun on a straight-in shot causes the cue ball to stop in place upon contacting the object ball. For every shot, you're going to have different options. That's what I love about the game, though: The mental part is so important. You've always got to be considering and turning options over in your mind. It's very therapeutic, because it shrinks the outside world into a smaller world where everything acts as the physics and mathematics dictate. I know it was the same for my dad. Playing pool was one of the only times he felt whole after coming back from the war.

Dad had a way of focusing and shutting everything else out when he came to a pool table. He wasn't thinking about his injuries or where his next paycheck would come from. He did the same thing when he was working on fixing something. He'd get so quiet, meticulously taking out screws and placing them neatly where he could keep track of them or changing out an engine part. You could see his determination to figure out what he was trying to fix and his confidence that he could. It didn't matter what it was—car brakes, a computer, a VCR, business paperwork, or an old radio—he knew he could figure out how to fix it, or else he knew whom to ask to teach him.

Whether he had a single tough shot or a clean break, you would see him lock in and "clear the mechanism" as he approached a pool table. His mind was already looking for the best pattern to run the table. And he always had confidence he could.

Incremental Improvement

In her book *Everything Is Figureoutable*, business and life coach Marie Forleo tells the story of her mom (who I think was a lot like my dad) taking apart a little Tropicana orange radio she loved when the antenna broke, and the tuner dial was a little off. Over the years she'd seen her mom take on dozens of things she'd never done before, from fixing a leak in the roof to retiling the bathroom.

"Hey, Mom," she asked her, "how do you know how to do so many things that you've never done before, without anyone showing you how to do it?"

Her mom put down her screwdriver and looked at her daughter. "Nothing in life is that complicated," she said. "You can do whatever you set your mind to if you just roll up your sleeves, get in there, and do it. Everything is figureoutable."[11]

In many ways, Ms. Forleo has built a business—and a life—on those very words.

You don't have to dig too deeply into the business leadership literature of the last couple of decades to come across the concept of *kaizen* and "The Toyota Way." *Kaizen* literally means "change for the better," or what a lot of thought leaders call "continuous improvement." It is one of the policies behind how Toyota became a top international brand from a mediocre one by continually asking the question, "How can we do [insert a process or practice] just a little bit better?" Over time, one tiny change at a time, it transformed the company and the cars that they made. It is one of the reasons Toyota is still a top car brand today.

This is also a habit Stephen Covey endorsed, what he called "sharpening the saw." It was the principle that taking care of your tools—or skills—is important to being more effective. In fact, it is his seventh habit, the one that makes the other six work. If you're not continually improving, making little things you do even easier and more effective, then you're not growing. If, instead, you improve every day just a little at a specific thing, you'll be surprised at how improved you will be at it by the end of a year. It's like the growth of a plant: You may not see a difference day to day, but at the end of a week or a month, it will look completely different. This is because of slow, steady, tortoise-rather-than-the-hare growth.

For Dad, the fundamentals of doing anything were obviously a little different because he only had one hand to hold something and one leg to stand on, but that's where he got creative. When he first began playing pool at the VA hospital as he recovered there, he rested the cue on the rail, but of course that was slippery, especially when shooting with English. Then he started to use the bridge more frequently, but that was awkward as well because it meant he needed to carry two cue sticks around with him with one hand, pretty much all the time. Eventually, he made his own bridge with a shorter handle to make it easier to carry and started playing with that all the time. It was light, though, and would sometimes slip.

About a year after he got back to Greeley, one of the guys at Dutch's saw him playing either off the rail or using his modified bridge and got an idea. The next day he came back with a bridge he had made out of brass without a cue stick connected to it. He had also put a felt bottom on it to reduce the slipping. Dad could take that and place it anywhere on the table and it would stay in place. Dad was thrilled, but that's when his tinkering creativity came alive.

The two of them started experimenting with the weight, height, and shape of this little portable bridge.

Dad sanded down the brass to make it smoother and keep the cue from sometimes catching against it, putting a bind on the shaft, and making the bridge slip. They also tried making it out of other materials, like foam or plastic, but he never liked those because they could never get them to be the right weight to stay in place.

He also tried using what is called a spider bridge. It has different slots for different angles, but it never felt right to Dad. There wasn't enough reason not to use a regular bridge for those shots anyway, but it did give him another idea.

Dad using his custom bridge

In the end, the bridge he developed had four slots with different heights, and another so that he could turn it on its side for maximum height. Which one he used depended on what type of English he wanted to put on the cue ball. Once he had it close to what he wanted, he made a little spot in his crutch where it would fit and he could carry it around and keep the cue stick in his other hand.

When he broke, he had to snatch the bridge up off the table so that it wouldn't interfere with any of the balls. He got really good at this. Boy, was he fast. Eventually he made one with a rosewood handle and a brass bridge that he would bring with him and use just for breaking and making longer shots. This gave him something more to grab after he broke, and the rest of the time he could leave it against the wall and use the more portable bridge stashed in a slot in his crutch.

Since there was still a need for shooting off of the rail every once in a while, Dad came up with the idea of making a little bean bag with some rubber cement strips on the bottom that he could place on the rail. For certain shots, he would rest his cue stick on it to help him keep his aim steady.

The whole process was super-creative.

He had the same attitude about business.

Just a few weeks ago we found an old box in his basement as we were going through his things. It was filled with floppy discs labeled "New Spanish Releases," "Action Movies," "Kid's Shows," and the like. It had to be from when Uncle Leo wanted to open a video store. He had asked Dad to partner with him.

It was Dad, though, who got it going. He organized all the movies, inventoried them, and figured out a way to check them out and get them checked back in, how to charge late fees, and all of that without using a computer originally and having no more than a box for cash. I remember when we built the shelves for it in our garage, and my sisters and I helped paint them blue.

Dad holding his first grandchild, my niece Vanessa, at the video store

When we got a new movie, we'd create a new case for it, put the name on the spine, and then file it alphabetically on custom shelves he made for behind the desk. We'd take the original case with the cover art on it, put Styrofoam in it, shrink-wrap it, and place it on the rental shelf in the proper genre section. When someone rented a video, we would swap them out and record the rental. If someone asked about a specific film, we could scan through the shelves behind the desk and see immediately which videos were out and which should be on a rental shelf. I remember the systems well, because my sisters and I were in our teens at the time and worked in the store. We would all take turns being there to check things in and out with my mom, Uncle Frank, and Aunt Teresa (who eventually partnered with my parents on the store), but it was Dad who developed all the systems needed for the business to run.

Eventually we got a computer, and Dad assigned every video a number, and its information was recorded. He used this to develop a way to keep track of what was renting the most and the least. When movies weren't renting, he collected a couple dozen of them and went to Denver to trade them for newer ones he thought people would want. He might trade four or five to get one, but it was better than having unrented videos taking up space on the shelves. The boxes we found brought back all these memories.

That was all Dad. That was him applying the knowledge, wisdom, and understanding that God gave him. That's what he lived by.

So many people get discouraged and quit before they even try. My dad was never like that. He'd take on tough jobs all the time, and then if he couldn't figure it out, he'd find someone to figure it out with. If he wanted to figure something out, he would. I do my best every day to live up to his example.

SEVEN

Courage

> Courage means boldly doing what you're afraid of, even though you stay scared the whole time you're doing it.
> —Manuel Gonzales Jr.

My dad's injuries came from an attack early in the evening of May 14, 1968. I only finally found out the details of how Dad was injured when I spoke to Don Fuller, the man who pulled him out of his track after it got hit and Dad always credited with saving his life. I first met Don when I was in my mid-twenties. I had a stucco job to do in Saginaw, Michigan, at the time. My dad had been in contact with Don and knew that Don lived near Saginaw. When my dad learned that I was going to Saginaw for work, he arranged for me and Don to meet each other at the hotel where I was staying.

I remember that day vividly. I was on my phone with my dad coming down the hotel stairs when I saw a man at the front desk. The man, Don Fuller, turned toward me, and at the moment he saw me, he started crying, having no doubt that I was my dad's son. We hugged and chatted a little but never talked about the war or how my dad got hurt. It wasn't until I approached Don in 2023, asking if I could interview him for this book, that he was gracious enough to share many details about his experience in Vietnam and that day that he saved my dad's life. I am forever grateful.

As was their routine when in the field, Don told me, the group was settling down for the night. For three days they had been chasing a unit of Viet Cong soldiers. A perimeter of concertina wire had been set up, and the first patrols were out. A Chinook helicopter had brought in a large tank of gasoline so they could pump fuel into the tracks. It was just before nightfall; there was only a little daylight left. Don Fuller had just refueled the Lucky 13 and pulled away, and Dad pulled in to refill Lulu.

Dad driving "Lulu"

I'm sure they must've experienced dozens of nights just like this one without incident, but as Dad had pulled his track away from the tank to park it for the night, the unit they had been following made a surprise counterattack. A rocket-propelled grenade came streaking out from the jungle tree line and hit Dad's track in the driver's corner. Dad told one reporter who interviewed him for an article that the impact probably would have killed him right away had he not turned around to check the ammo supply behind him in the track.

Suddenly everything was chaos as the entire platoon jumped to their feet and concentrated fire on the area the RPG had been fired from.

Don had the presence of mind to attend to Dad first and pull him out of the fire of the burning track. His leg and half of his arm were already gone, and he was badly burned all over. The exposed flesh was bloody and raw and sprayed with shrapnel wounds. Don couldn't remember how long things took in the chaos, but they got an emergency Red Cross chopper in, a Huey, and flew Dad back to the base for medical care as fast as they could. When his track was hit by the RPG, Dad must have thought that would be the end of him. Don said the firefight lasted throughout the rest of the night.

Dad in his army fatigues

COURAGE

In the early hours of the next morning, Myron "Pete" Peterson was out beyond the perimeter and had gotten shot in the hip and couldn't make it back. He called their commanding officer, but the officer didn't want to risk sending anyone after him as the fighting continued, so he told Myron to hang tight. Instead, Myron called Don. Don grabbed another guy, and they crawled out and dragged Myron back in with the other guy who was with him. The other guy was dead.

Once they were back, Myron went back to base camp by Huey as well.

Don saved at least two lives that night.

A week or so later, Don got hit in the mouth by a .50-caliber machine gun as it swung around, so he had to go to the base to see a dentist. He was scheduled to be flown back to his platoon the same day. He said he'd never spent a night at a base except on first arrival and right before he went home. He was on active duty somewhere in the field the rest of his time on duty.

Having some time before his flight back, Don went to the medical facility to check in on Dad. He was in bad shape. The doctor didn't expect him to survive, but his heart kept on beating. When Don entered his room, Dad was sleeping. He roused and looked right at Don. When Dad saw him, Dad asked, "Why did you do it? Why did you save me, man?"

It was obvious to Don at least part of him was wishing he hadn't survived, that he didn't think any of the rest of his life would be worth living with the extent of his injuries and the pain he was experiencing.

Don had no answer for him. Even though he knew he'd done the right thing, it hurt. He almost fell apart.

Still, Dad survived and was flown home. Before he left, the doctor told my dad he was one strong, determined man to have lived through what he did.

The Courage to Heal

In his book *Courage: Winning Life's Toughest Battles*, Edwin Louis Cole tells the story of talking to a young man who was confused about the relationship between ambition and humility. Mr. Cole writes:

> He wanted to be godly, but at the same time he wanted to be successful in business and reap the financial rewards. . . .
>
> "Don't kill your ego," I told [him], " . . . Direct it. Channel it. Purify your motives and use your ego to achieve great things for God."[12]

To me, my dad was always humble but never timid. A lot of people confound the two, but Dad knew how to balance them. Dad kept his priorities in order, but he also kept his wants simple. He only found a couple ways to relax—to play pool and to fix or build things—and work that plugged into those and his need to use his tools and his mind. People mattered to him, especially family, and by making serving others the goal of most of his activities, he kept things in proper perspective. He always loved a good challenge, whether it was on the pool table, in his shop, or talking someone through a tough spot in their life.

People seemed to look up to him because it was obvious he had overcome some tough stuff. He demanded a sense of respect for his duty to his country, his attitude, and the person he was. He loved people. And despite his handicap, he was hard to feel sorry for, because he carried such an appreciation of the life he had.

You might be able to beat Dad in a game, but you couldn't discourage him. Every time he'd play—win, lose, or draw—he was always the same: his smiling, happy-go-lucky, friendly self. He was always a great opponent. If he lost, he was respectful and congratulatory, and if he won, he was humble and just as respectful. He always built the other player up, no matter what. He didn't sweat the small stuff. He was very hard to offend.

He wouldn't let anyone say anything bad about a family member or teammate, but for the most part, he let remarks roll off him without much reaction, even when people got a little bent out of shape about something. As I said before, he didn't like it when people didn't take him seriously as an opponent, but that was something he responded to with his play, not his words. Maybe it was more because he aways wanted to see people perform at their best more than anything else. Whether the person across the table from him was semipro or playing their first tournament, he'd treat them the same.

At the same time, he was never beaten until the last ball dropped. He was always hopeful, and he always believed that, given the chance, he could run the table. If he was given another chance, he'd take it—if not, well, that's just the way the balls roll sometimes. He'd shake the other person's hand, turning his left hand upside down to grasp theirs, and congratulate them. Sometimes people didn't know how to take that. They would reach out naturally, and then remember he didn't have a right hand, and then drop their hand unsure of what to do. Dad would then give them a little laugh to put them at ease and reach out his left hand upside down to shake their right hand. His response was always in love.

A top Colorado player and one of the guys on our championship team in 2006, Chris McDaniel, said the thing he appreciated the most about Dad was his grace. He said Dad was always respectful and never sour. He never wanted things to get heavy, never took himself too seriously, and was always complimenting other players to build them up.

Getting good at playing pool is a challenge enough for anyone, let alone someone having to stand on one leg and play with the opposite hand from what they had grown up favoring. It takes a degree of courage to sign up for a tournament, especially to spend the money to travel to attend one. It's certainly a test of nerves. It also takes courage to start your own business, like Dad did with the video store and other ventures. And it certainly takes courage to sign up to serve your country in a war.

But a lot of that is also the courage to break out of a rut and create something better for yourself. Without courage, we get stuck. I know Dad had a lot of anxiety after the war, and I remember sometimes seeing him in his chair, sleeping, having bad dreams. I know pool became an outlet for him to get away from the horrible things he had experienced, as did fixing things for other people. A layout of balls on a table was a puzzle he could solve. An Xbox or an engine or a model of some kind was a problem he could fix.

Later in life, when he couldn't get around as well, he turned to making complicated LEGO structures. He had shelves and shelves of them. My niece, Mariah, remembers he used to let her help him organize the shelves as high as she could reach when she was younger. Later he let her help him organize car parts, drone parts, or whatever he was working on in his workshop. She loved trying to figure out what he was thinking as he made things. She was always amazed how he knew every part, what it did, where it fit, and how he could explain all of that to her in a way she could understand.

Dad putting together a LEGO model

Dad was always keeping busy, being of service to others, and being constructive in some way. At one point he even had a little train set village all set out that he had collected over time and built little structures for. All of these things helped him deal with the trauma of what he had experienced that was both horrible and he had no control over. It's good to have things that you can control and to create something to show for your skills, whether it be a fixed-up car or a tournament trophy.

He never did anything halfway. I think after he opened his first VCR, it wasn't a month before he had dozens sitting in line to be fixed next. He went from his first kit to hundreds of LEGO models in about a year. He built helicopters, boats, Batman vehicles, *Star Wars* figures and ships. When he passed away, he was in the middle of a LEGO *Star Wars* model that had over thirteen thousand pieces. There are still shelves of the models he made over the years in my mom's living room.

Dad was also a bit of a trailblazer in how he stood up for other players. Back when most pool halls frowned on women playing, he welcomed them and encouraged them to play by teaching them. He taught my Aunt Kathy to play, and she eventually won a trophy. She remembered being in a bar in Greeley playing against the bar owner's daughter, and Dad was there cheering her on. It was down to the eight ball in a corner pocket, but there were balls between the cue ball and the eight. Dad coached her on where to aim for the kick shot, and she sank it. She was such a fan of his that she went to Las Vegas when he received his jacket and induction into the VNEA Hall of Fame. She was so excited to see him honored.

Kathy Farmer, who became a family friend, had a similar experience when she was growing up and wanted to learn the game. "Girls weren't very welcome at the pool hall then," she told me. Dad was one of the first guys to talk with her, teach her about the game, and give her tips on how to conduct herself when playing. When guys saw him do that, they accepted her as a player. My dad and Kathy even played in a Scotch Doubles tournament in Las Vegas one time. Dad had played eight-ball all day, but when he saw Kathy wanted to play, he asked her if she'd partner with him. Matches didn't even start till 10 p.m., and the finals wouldn't be until 3 a.m., but Dad didn't complain about being tired. He joked with her to help her nerves and was cheery all the way through. They didn't win, but it was something Kathy never forgot. She showed up when he was inducted into the Hall of Fame as well. A lot of people from Colorado went down to Vegas just for that.

Honestly, I don't think human beings are built for the horrors and trauma of war. Like a lot of veterans, Dad's experiences deeply affected him, but he didn't want to let it show to anyone else, especially his kids. It takes courage to get help for such things, and it takes courage to step up and help yourself. I think Dad worked a lot of his trauma out through his projects and play, and he learned to value every person and experience that came his way. He savored family, friends, competition, work, and life more than any other person I have ever known. He knew how to be content with what he had even as he worked for more. He faced life with a courage I've always tried to emulate. He was certainly a hero to me, the rest of our family, and many others.

Calculating the Tangent Line

I think Dad was at his best teaching pool, though. I remember one of the things he was really patient with me about was understanding the tangent line.

Once you master your shot routine—your stance, aim, grip, bridge, stroke, staying down, and following through—it's time to start thinking about where the cue ball will end up after your present shot to make your next shot easier. Doing that demands mastering the mathematics of the tangent line, the line the cue ball will take after contacting the object ball. It's conquering this that transitions someone from being a casual player into becoming an amateur—a true lover of the game.

As I mentioned before, using stun on a straight-in shot will cause the cue ball to stop in place upon contact with the object ball. Using stun on cut shots causes the cue ball to head along the tangent line—a ninety-degree angle from the line of the object ball to the pocket—after contacting the object ball. The harder you hit the cue ball, the farther it will travel along the tangent line before forward roll starts to kick in and causes the cue ball to break off the tangent line away from you.

This is where you can start to use that knowledge to really control the cue ball. Using high English, hitting the cue ball in or above the center, will cause the cue ball to start down the tangent line after contacting the object ball and then break off the line away from you. Low English (hitting the bottom of the cue ball below stun) will cause the cue ball to start down the tangent line and then break off toward you. The length of time that the cue ball stays on the tangent line and the degree that it breaks off the line are dependent upon how hard and how high or low you strike the cue ball.

Calculating the tangent line is the first tool that will let you begin to think three shots ahead, because it's about where the cue ball will go after it strikes the object ball. It's probably the most difficult concept for most beginners to get used to and comfortable with. You've got to calculate and follow that tangent line in your mind, and then play off it. Once you see the tangent line, then it's a matter of controlling speed, English, and slight adjustments in your contact point on the object ball to get the cue ball into position to shoot your next shot.

One way to practice this is to take fourteen balls and place them against the long rails next to the diamonds, or dots (this will include in front of the two side pockets as well but not the corners). Then take the cue ball and the remaining object ball and set up different shots to make so that the cue ball will tangent off the object ball into each ball in succession along the rails. Shoot each shot with stun so that you can learn where the natural tangent line is. The more you practice this, the more you'll start automatically seeing the tangent line. Eventually this line becomes so automatic you stop thinking about it and can then focus instead on the magnitude of how to strike it and how much spin you'll need to get it to end up where you'd like it.

I remember watching Dad shoot the same shot over and over again, adjusting his speed and high and low English to see what they would do to the tangent line. Each iteration gave him a better understanding of what was possible. He took the same principle into life, staying curious, exploring different ways to do things, always asking questions.

The game really begins to get fun as you open up the options for how to make shots and set up the next ones. That's when the physics of the game becomes really cool, because that's when your creativity starts to come into play with the natural laws of the table. When you start getting your skills to work together with the physics, it begins to feel as if there's no shot that can't be made.

Some of His Best Shots Ever

Over the years, Dad made some remarkable shots in his pool career. He walked me through one he made one time so I could understand his approach. He was facing the table the long way, and the cue ball was about two inches off the left-hand side pocket. The object ball was about the same distance off the rail with a shot that was straight into the corner pocket. The ball he wanted to set up to shoot next was about the same distance off the rail on the other side of the table.

Most people would approach this as a straight shot and feel like they had no chance to get position on the next ball. Instead, he hit it with low right English and bounced the cue ball off the rail before it contacted the object ball. It hit the object ball where he wanted, sending it down into the far corner pocket, and then the low right English spun the cue ball to the rail on the other side of the table to set up the next shot.

One time he was playing in a tournament, and he was on the last ball before the eight. The only path available to get position on the eight ball would require him to send the cue ball three rails. The problem was that there were a lot of the opponent's balls creating traffic to pass through. Hitting any of the opponent's balls would have altered the path and position on the eight. He put high left English on the cue ball with a long follow-through. When the English took, it cleared five or six other balls, not touching any of them, and lined up perfectly on the eight. The guy he was playing looked at him blankly. "How'd you do that?"

COURAGE

Dad going for the win

Another time he was playing a friend who had just tied up the match. It was Dad's shot, but his opponent wasn't worried because there was a cluster of balls he would have to deal with before he would be able to get a shot on any of the balls in the group. However, he had a pretty easy shot to the corner. Looking over his options, he ended up firing it hard into the corner sinking that ball, and then the cue ball went three rails and laid into the bunch and broke them up. He even told his friend what he was going to do before he shot it, and his friend just scoffed. It had to be perfect, and it was. His friend freaked out. The cue ball sank the object ball, cut a figure eight on the table, and then broke up the bunch, giving Dad multiple options for shots. It was beautiful.

When I was sixteen, he and I were always going to tournaments together. We were both sort of in our primes in those days. He was playing at the AAA level. It was a state tournament, and he was having a lot of fun because he was in stroke. I could always tell when he was playing really well because he'd be joking and laughing a little more than usual. He acted as if he couldn't miss a shot.

It was getting down to the final rounds, and he was playing a top northern Colorado player, Dino Devost, who wouldn't give him many chances to get back into the game if he missed. He had a shot where he needed to put extreme low English on the ball for a draw shot, but the cue ball was just off the end rail and surrounded by other balls that made the cue ball look impossible to get to. It was in this little window, probably only three inches by three inches, that he had to escape. The object ball was in the middle of the table, so he'd also have to hit the cue ball with some force to get it there and with a ton of low spin to clear everything else.

He took a step back from the table and held the cue stick in his left hand, almost like a dart or spear. His only chance was to cut the object ball into one of the corner pockets, but either way it would have to low spin to avoid a scratch and/or running into other balls.

It looked absolutely impossible.

His shot clipped the object ball at just the right angle, sending it into the far corner pocket, and the cue ball avoided the scratch, the other balls, and left him straight in on the eight ball.

The crowd gasped. No one had ever seen anything like it.

Everybody was surprised. How did he do that? In fact, one of my friends came over and asked, "How did he do that?" I shook my head in disbelief, with the biggest smile on my face and eyes wide open in surprise. "I have no idea," I answered.

It was the shot of the tournament and the one that allowed him to go on and win it all, because he easily sank the eight after that and moved on to the final round. It was the most focused I think I ever saw him play. It may have been because that was probably also the best field of players he'd ever faced. He was in a zone all his own. He made some other pretty spectacular shots that tournament, but that was the best—in fact, it was the best shot I can remember him ever making. Looking back, I'm so glad I got to be there for it!

EIGHT

Respect Yourself and Others

Every person counts the same.
—Manuel Gonzales Jr.

Mom was cleaning a patient's room at the hospital when someone came to her and told her the head nurse wanted to see her. She had no idea what it was about. She stopped what she was doing and went to the nurses' station. The head nurse told her Dad had gotten hurt and was on his way to a hospital in Japan as soon as he was stable enough. She didn't have any more details for her than that.

Then followed some tense months of waiting with little news.

Finally, in August, Dad was moved to William Beaumont General Hospital in El Paso, Texas. My Grandma Mary; Dad's paternal grandmother, Louise; Uncle Leo; and my mom got into a car and drove to see him the day he was to arrive. Aunt Pauline drove down with Grandma Mary's brother Louis; his wife, Sadie Pisano; and some of their kids. They spent a night in Juarez and went to see him the next day.

Mom remembers walking through a hospital filled with nineteen-, twenty-, and twenty-one-year-olds, all now invalids from the war. Many were missing limbs. It was like no hospital she had ever seen before. Every bed was full, and many were making their way around in wheelchairs or on crutches.

The doctors would only let one of them into the room at a time to see Dad. Grandma Mary went first. When Dad found out who else was there, he told her he didn't want my mom to come in to see him. He said to tell her he released her from marrying him. She should go back to Greeley and marry someone else who was whole. Uncle Leo went in next, and Dad told him the same thing.

When Leo told this to my mom, she wouldn't have any of it. She told Leo, "Take me to his room."

After Dad had left to go back to camp before Vietnam, my mom had wondered about their engagement. She had been engaged before, of course, and she wondered, *How could I have told a man I only really knew for two weeks that I would marry him?* But in that moment, when Uncle Leo told her she should leave without seeing him, she resolved to go in. She felt that something in her had changed.

The stumps left of Dad's arm and leg were wrapped in balls of white gauze about the size of basketballs. His face was pocked with black scars left from the shrapnel. He poked at them, trying to dig them out. What was worse, though, was the broken look on his face. Mom told me, "When I saw him lying in the bed, God let me know that I loved him."

Dad told her he didn't want to marry her anymore. He said she was a good girl and deserved a whole man. But she told him, "But I love you. I don't want to be with nobody but you."

I feel like that moment changed Dad forever. In the coming months, as they wrote back and forth, he still encouraged her to go out—to go see shows, to go out dancing, etc.—and see if she didn't really want to marry someone else, but she always refused. She would wait, she wrote back. She'd go out with her girlfriends, but she wasn't going to date anyone.

I think when Dad learned that Mom still loved him despite his injuries, it gave him permission to be whole in a way a lot of people who are physically whole never realize. I don't know if it was exactly how he thought about it, but it was like he felt the injuries and the war were the worst things that could ever happen to him in his life, so it was all downhill from there. His attitude began to change. His injuries hadn't beaten him, so nothing else ever could. There was nothing he would face in the future that he couldn't figure out. There wasn't a person he wasn't glad to get the chance to meet. There were completely new things to live for.

Mom had given him a new beginning.

Dad home from Vietnam

Finding His Way Forward

Dad always stuck out wherever he went because of his missing arm and leg, especially in a pool hall. People noticed him, and then he would greet them in his casual way. Then once they noticed how good he was, they would want to talk with him. He was a local celebrity, and because he was also so friendly, everyone got to know him. He knew the value of a life and was always interested in seeing people reach their potential. He was kind and patient with people, especially as a teacher. He was always smiling and seemed to have an aura of approachability about him. If he smiled at you, you couldn't not smile back. It was infectious.

He used to randomly invite people he met home. I don't suppose it hurt that my mom was a great cook. She would cook twice a day, and she would make fresh flour tortillas for each meal. There's nothing like fresh flour tortillas; it's nothing like what you can get at a store. It isn't even close. We used to use them instead of silverware. You'd rip off a piece of it and you'd grab your food with it and eat. No fork needed.

It wasn't Mexican food like what you'd get from Mexico either. People get confused. It wasn't carne asada tacos and barbacoa. What we grew up on, I'd call it more like Chicano-style food, where it was fresh flour tortillas, not corn tortillas. Fresh pinto beans, a big breakfast, a lot of eggs and bacon, chorizo, pork green chili, chicken molé, homemade beef burritos smothered with pork green chili, and homemade sopapillas. She was and still is most known for her "Gomez Enchiladas," which she learned to make from her mom, my Grandma Esther Gomez.

Gomez Enchiladas are made with a mix of Jimmy Dean sausage, red potatoes, and mild cheddar cheese rolled up in a flour tortilla and smothered with molé and more cheese. My dad used to add butter, chili pequin, and fresh diced onions to the top. Over the years, I watched tons of our friends try them, and I never met anyone who didn't love them and come back for more. It's what a lot of them referred to as Mexican food, but not the Mexican food that you'd get from a Mexican restaurant nowadays. So we were pretty spoiled growing up.

I think Dad was proud of her cooking, and anybody and everybody who had ever tried a tortilla fell in love with my mom's food. So maybe part of why he was always inviting people home for dinner was he wanted to show off a little. I don't know. I know I definitely did when I invited friends over and would be excited for them to try my mom's food because it was very, very good.

A big part of community for my dad was eating meals together. He would invite people over to the house all the time, and if we went to a tournament out of town, we'd always end up all together in a restaurant talking late into the evening. If they came over to the house, it was really homey, and I think guests felt that. Dad was great at asking questions and getting people to talk about themselves and the things they cared about. Maybe a small part of that was not wanting to talk so much about himself or his past. Listening to those conversations, I think I learned more about their past from them than I ever did about my dad's past in five conversations with him. To find out about Vietnam, I had to talk with people who had gone over with him or were at boot camp with him.

Growing up, I remember there used to be a place called J Watson's, where Dad played all the time, and before I was old enough to play pool, the owner used to let me play in the arcade for free. That was when I first started seeing the relationship my dad had with the owners of places and realized he was pretty popular.

Wally Howton became Dad's best friend when I was growing up. He once told Dad he collected cookie jars. Since Dad was always at yard sales looking for antiques to fix up and resell, every time Dad saw a unique-looking cookie jar, he would buy it for him. Because of Dad's thoughtfulness and generosity, they became fast friends. He was always doing little things like that.

In Las Vegas at the VNEA International Championships, he was so well-known that he wouldn't be able to walk more than a couple of steps without someone wanting to shake his hand. Everyone stopped to say hi.

When I was younger and playing, he would always try to lighten things up if I got too serious. At the same time, he wouldn't let me get too superficial. I remember when I got to be a top AAA player and we were both playing AAA, Dad wouldn't even let me goof around in practice. "Hey, you do not let up," he told me. "You stay focused, and you play your game." I was a teenager playing with adults, so he wanted me to focus on the game and not act my actual age. I learned that lesson double if we ever came up against each other in a draw. He beat me in plenty of tournaments. He was always rooting for me, but if I was going to beat him, I'd have to earn it.

The first time I did actually beat him in a tournament was a real milestone for me. It felt good to beat someone I knew was good. He was so proud of me.

When I was fourteen, my dad entered me into a VNEA state singles tournament. I was playing at the C level. It was all men in the tournament. I had a match against a friend of Dad's, a guy named Pat Whalan, and we were three to three in a best-of-seven match. The winner of this match moved on to the finals, and the loser was out of the tournament. The final game was a back-and-forth battle leaving only the eight ball left for both of us, but it was my turn. When I made it, all I remember is hearing Dad's voice screaming, "Yes!" in triumph from somewhere in the shadows around the table.

Dave Gross, a good friend and a well-known player around the country, said Dad taught him not to let limitations be limitations, and that you should face games in the same way you faced hardships, with no excuses, a smile on your face, treating everyone with dignity and being a good sport. Winning with people was always more important than winning at pool.

This was something he had to teach me again and again. When I was younger and he was teaching me, I think that might have been the most fun I had playing pool. There were no expectations, so every shot I made was a triumph. Then as I got older and started competing, making shots only mattered if I was winning games. Then, after I won a tournament or two, it was only winning tournaments that mattered. I let the pressure mount, and I began to see how hard I would have to work to get good enough to play at higher levels or even maybe go pro someday.

Dad kept all of that in perspective for me, though. In those days, there wasn't a living to be made playing pool, even if I did go pro. The guys who made it to that level spent all their money going from place to place to compete—to really prosper, they had to have most of their income come from someplace else.

That's why I started my company at nineteen. I had made a choice. Rather than wanting to be a professional player who didn't have much income, I chose, like my dad, to be an entrepreneur and still a pretty good pool player. My decision paid off. While learning and growing a business, I was still able to win countless state tournaments at the highest amateur level and also a couple of amateur international championships. In 2006, after winning the Valley National 8-Ball League Association (VNEA) International Masters team event and placing fifth in the Masters singles, I decided to stop playing altogether and focus on my family and business. Although most of my friends and family were confused by my decision, my dad understood and supported me.

It wasn't until recently, now that my kids are grown, that I've felt I could come back to the game and appreciate it for what it is. With a nice tight-pocket Diamond pool table downstairs, I have time to practice and enjoy the game again. For the first time in a long time, I feel I'm able to live up to the level of fun Dad always seemed to enjoy so naturally. Now I can let fun be the main part of the game again. In fact, when I told him I was going to get a table and start playing again, maybe even try to go pro, he said, "Just make sure you have fun at it." It's a piece of advice I think of every time I pick up a pool cue.

I've never met anyone who had a bad thing to say about my dad. It was always the opposite. When people learned who I was, they'd go out of their way to say good things about him.

My mom recommended a restaurant in Greeley one time, and when my family went, I casually mentioned that my mom had recommended them.

"Who's your mom?" the owner asked me.

"Dolores Gonzales," I answered.

"So your dad's Manuel Gonzales, the pool player?"

"Yes," I told him.

He spent the next ten minutes telling me how much he respected him and how amazing and kind he was.

That even happened in Saginaw, Michigan, one time. (A similar thing happened in Texas too.) I was there for work, and a buddy and I got into a money game in a bar. I was wearing a Broncos jersey, and some guy asked, "You guys from Colorado?"

"Yeah," I answered.

"You guys ever go to tournaments in Vegas?"

"Yeah."

"The only guy I know from Colorado that I met there is this one-armed, one-legged guy who plays pretty good. He's the most amazing person I've ever seen."

I laughed. "Yeah," I told him. "That's my dad."

This started to become pretty common in the pool world and happened again at a tournament in Cheyenne. Some friends and I were waiting at the hotel bar for the tournament to start. The bartender asked if we were there for the tournament. We said we were. She said that she had recently been to Match Ups Pool Hall in Fort Collins and saw one of the most amazing things she had ever seen in her life. There was a guy there playing pool who only had one arm and one leg.

I decided to have some fun this time. "No way!" I responded. "I don't know if I believe you. That's impossible!" When my friends started laughing, she knew something was up, so I confessed that that guy was my dad.

The Good Life

The Good Life, by Robert Waldinger and Marc Schulz, chronicles a study on Harvard graduates and a selection of men in the Boston area regarding happiness and quality of life. It's been going on since

1938; it now includes women as well and is into its third generation of participants.

Among the amazing things this study has uncovered are lessons such as this: "The good life is joyful ... and challenging. Full of love, but also pain. And it never strictly *happens*; instead, the good life *unfolds*, through time."[13] Another is that money, fame, and cool possessions are not what makes a great life—genuine friendship is! "People who are more connected to family, to friends, and to community, are happier and physically healthier than people who are less well connected."[14]

One of the things I feel Dad did best was make friends and then gather them into a vital community. They'd come for the pool lessons but stay for the life lessons. We played together, we ate together, we laughed together, and at Dad's memorial service, they came and we cried together.

Dad gathered people around him because he knew that sometimes in the world we live in, the only place of refuge is in a group of friends. Men don't make friends like women do. My mom had a way of gathering friends around cooking and taking care of kids and going to church. Women do things face-to-face. Men, on the other hand, do things side by side—watching sports together, working on something like an engine, or playing a game. Some people have poker groups; Dad gathered a community around pool tables. But we didn't just play together; we did life together.

Dad always offered what he knew freely. He may not have done it intentionally, but through his openness, he found people who needed friends and taught them how to be friends. He was a person others could depend on, and he taught them how to be dependable. In teaching them how to see relationships on a pool table differently, he taught them how to see relationships in life differently as well. Everyone who was part of that community benefited from it, and a lot of us learned how to grow up to be responsible human beings in it as well. Dad was our example.

Using the Rail

Dad taught me several "kick shot" and "bank shot" systems for using the rails. What is a kick shot? A kick shot is when you are contacting a rail with the cue ball before contacting your object ball. Each diamond along the rail (a lot of modern tables just have dots instead of the old diamonds, but they are for the same purpose) has a value, your cue ball has a value, and then there's a mathematical equation to decide where to hit the cue ball for whichever angle you want.

All the diamonds are connected mathematically. There are certain systems that let you know, if the cue is at one diamond, which corresponding diamond on the opposite side you need to hit to send the cue ball or object ball, one rail, two rails, or even three rails or more.

The typical measure for a basic one-rail kick shot is two to one. Let's say you're shooting from just outside the side pocket and you want the cue ball to bounce off the opposite rail and hit an object ball that is hanging in the corner pocket on the same side of the table. In this case, you have four diamonds between the object ball and cue ball. The idea is that if you shoot the cue ball two diamonds down from the opposite side pocket, it will hit four diamonds down on your side of the table, where the object ball is. If there were three diamonds of separation in between, you would then hit one and a half diamonds down from directly across the opposite side. The idea behind this system is that the angle going into the rail is the same as the angle coming off—two to one.

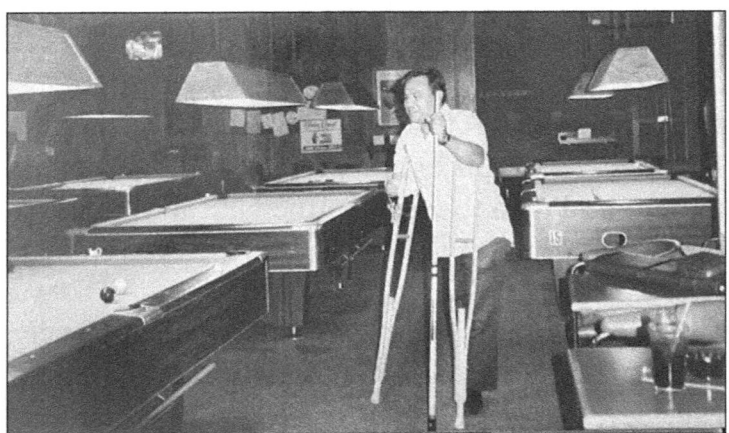

Dad admiring an opponent's shot

Basic two-rail kick shots can be safer and more efficient than one-rail kick shots because the formula is even more precise. For basic two-rail kick shots, you need to stand behind the shot line toward the rail you will be hitting first. Then you need to find the midpoint between the cue ball and object ball, drawing a line into the corner pocket next to the first rail to be contacted with the cue ball. Once you find that line, all you need to do is parallel shift that line back to the cue ball, and then you have your aim line. Depending on the table and how hard you hit the cue ball, you will need to add a little "running" English. Running English is spin toward the angle off the rail to be hit first. It will take practice with speed and calculating the English but is a great system for two-rail kick shots.

For three-rail kick shots, it's best to start learning by shooting out of a corner pocket and aiming about a diamond and a half past the side pocket on the opposite long rail with running English. If at first your cue ball comes up short of the corner pocket, you can start moving your aim-line down the rail. If you're coming up long, you can move your aim-line closer to the side pocket. The amount of spin and how hard you hit the cue ball will also affect how the cue ball comes off the rails, so keep experimenting and find what works best for you.

Bank Shots

A bank shot is when you shoot the object ball into a rail to try to make it bounce off into a certain pocket. It's basically the same two-to-one concept, except instead of calculating where the cue ball should hit the rail, you're angling the object ball to hit the desired spot.

Dad showed me how a basic bank shot is pretty much the same as a one-rail kick shot. The idea is that the object ball is going to have the same angle coming off the rail as it did going into the rail. Again, different speeds affect the rebound angle on a bank shot, so you will need to practice your bank shots with different magnitudes to see how this works.

With any kick or bank shot, the harder you hit the cue ball, the more the cue ball is going to compress that rail, and then it's going to come off more sharply and the angle will be tighter, bringing the ball back closer to you. Different kinds of English will affect this in different ways as well. Tables with older rails may play differently, and some even unevenly. As I said before, you're playing the table, so you have to figure out how its rails play. You have to take all of these things into consideration as you set up your shots. But once you can accurately calculate these angles, you can use kicks and banks to your advantage.

If you want to practice this, you might want to take some golf tees, or something similar, to set them upside down on the rails atop the diamonds to help you remember which one you're shooting at each time and then try different speeds and mark where they hit with different-colored tees.

Dad's favorite bank shot was a side-pocket bank shot using the short rail that was so automatic, Kathy Farmer dubbed it the "Manuel bank." I have never really seen anyone else do it, but Dad used to do it all the time.

In today's pool world, there are many banking and kicking systems that work great. There's not enough room to cover all of them here, but just knowing that they exist is more than most players even consider. And there are certainly enough videos on YouTube to get you started practicing each style. The more you practice these, the more you will naturally see them, and that gives you more options for shots and for which system you think matches your skills and knowledge the best.

Kindness Personified

My son Manuel IV once told me he never knew his grandfather to be idle; he was always doing something, but no matter what it was, he was never too busy to spend time or show him something. I know his grandpa always made time for family and was constantly checking up on them to make sure everyone was good.

My son also said that some of his favorite times with his grandfather were when he'd come home late at night and find him still up doing something. He would join him, and they would end up talking for hours about anything and everything, ranging from pool to when he would build and race model cars again. Before he knew it, it would be three or four in the morning. Dad always had time to spend with his family.

My dad was a very tenderhearted man. I remember when my Uncle Joe (my dad's youngest stepbrother) was in the hospital. Dad couldn't stop crying, even though all reports were Joe would be okay. I never thought they were that close since he was so much younger and from his mother's third marriage, but it definitely affected him. It was the first time I realized how much Dad loved all his siblings. Uncle Joe used to come with my grandma and watch him play downtown. Uncle Joe loved to watch his older brother play.

Encounters at tournaments could be difficult too. I remember one time, we were sitting around, and a drunk man came up to Dad and asked him if he'd gotten hurt in Vietnam. Dad told him yes.

"Well," he wanted to know, "how did it happen?"

"I don't like to talk about it," my dad answered.

Rather than accepting that, the guy continued to push.

I could tell it upset my dad because his voice got hoarse and his eyes watered up.

I was torn inside seeing this. I was probably about thirteen at the time, so although I wanted to, there was no way it would have done any good for me to tell this guy to leave my dad alone, but the other half of me wanted my dad to answer. I had always wondered what had happened to him, but he always refused to talk about it. Both options scared me.

Fortunately, Wally Howton was there, saw what was happening, and came over to distract the man. When the guy started to get loud, Wally called the pool officials over, and they removed the man from the tournament hall.

Tyson Brown, who was in Las Vegas with us numerous times, said Dad taught him, "No matter what happens in life, roll with the punches; be who you are, stay true to yourself, and don't let things get you down."

One funny thing happened when my sister Denise was in first grade. Her teacher set up a home conference with my parents to discuss an issue she was experiencing with Denise at school. When the teacher arrived at my parents' home, she was greeted by my mom. She explained to my mom that she noticed a pattern in Denise's drawings: her animals, tables, and chairs were all missing a leg. As she spoke, my dad walked in on his crutches. She took one look at my dad, and it all made sense. The teacher went from being concerned about Denise's perception of the world to finding a new love for her.

My sister Renee's favorite memory with my dad was when they danced together at her wedding. Dad was in his wheelchair at the time, and they started to dance with him sitting in it. Then their song came on, "Before the Next Teardrop Falls" by Freddy Fender. Halfway through it, Dad decided to stand up and finish the dance standing.

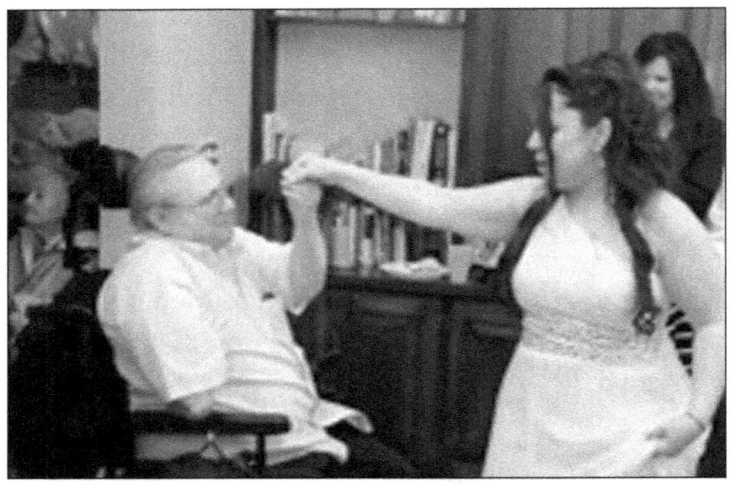

Dad dancing with my sister Renee at her wedding

We all remember Dad making cupcakes for birthdays, jumping on the trampoline with us, taking great vacations together, and so many other good memories. When Denise had her accounting final coming up, Dad bragged that he was the first to finish his accounting exam—finishing in a third of the allowed time—and got 100 percent on the final.

When Denise's first baby, Vanessa, was born, she came home to find their house ready for the new granddaughter with the drawers filled with baby clothes and the changing table filled with diapers.

When Denise and her family moved to Arizona, anytime Mom and Dad went to Las Vegas, a visit to Arizona was always part of the trip.

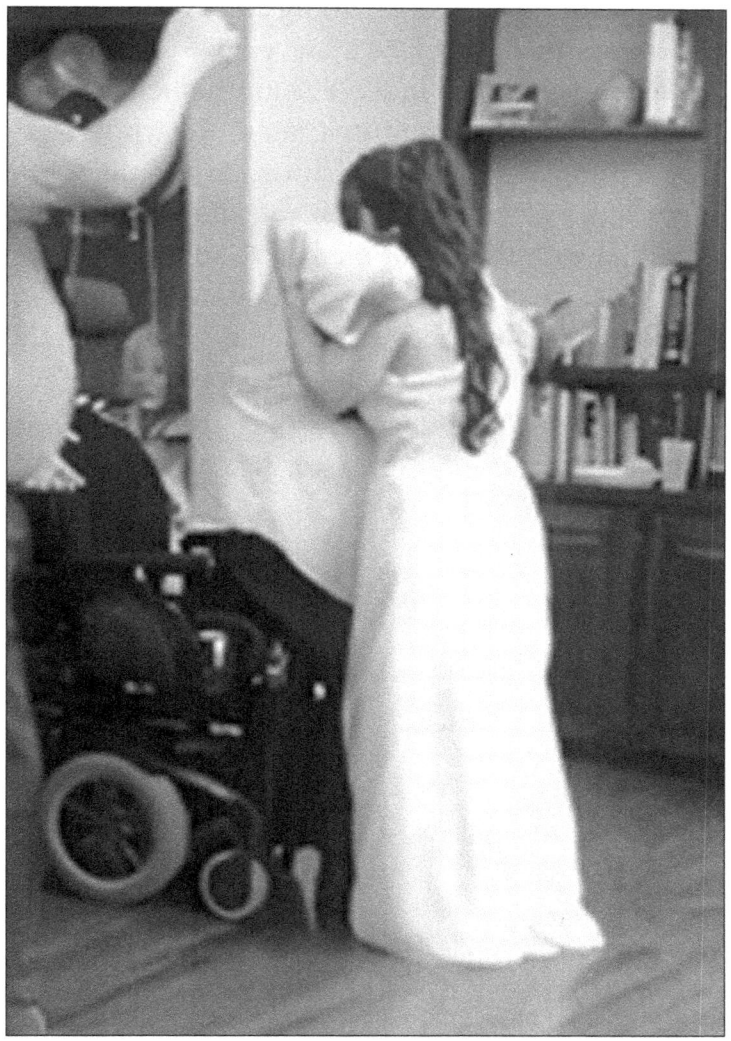

Dad stands out of his wheelchair to finish their dance

Joe Alvarez, who used to go to Las Vegas with us to play, remembered many hours sitting together with a cup of coffee in front of him, just talking and talking with Dad about anything and everything. He was always amazed at Dad's "never give up" attitude.

When we played in VNEA tournaments in Las Vegas, especially team tournaments, the whole team always hung out together. If someone said they were going to go get something to eat, the whole group would go with them. We'd all go to shows together. One time, one of the guys won some money, like three or four hundred dollars, and he bought the whole team dinner. He even rented a limousine, and everyone rode around town in it.

Dad's team the year before I joined. They were (the men, left to right) Terry "Weasel" Sharp, Dutch Klinginsmith (their sponsor), Tommy Martin, Dad, Danny Kendall, Ben Manzanares, Wally Howton, and Warren Woodson.

RESPECT YOURSELF AND OTHERS

If someone didn't have the money to go to Vegas with the team, a garage sale was organized, and everyone would bring something to sell to raise money for the trip. That's just the way things were done, and I always felt, in one way or another, Dad was usually behind it all.

José Loma, who became a top pool player, remembered watching Dad play when he was sixteen. He was amazed at how quickly Dad got around the table and set up his shots. "He showed me anything was possible," José once told me. "No matter what! Stay with it, and good things will happen."

Juan Euresti, one of my dad's closest friends who played with us a good deal, said Dad would light up a room with his smile, it was so infectious. Through all the years hanging out with my dad and playing with him, he never saw Dad down. People would smile when he came into a pool hall. He just had a way about him that made others better for being near him. He valued every person he met.

I certainly saw that as well. If anything, it's the characteristic of his I most want to carry and pass on to my kids. I can't think of a better legacy.

NINE

Why We Play

There's no point in playing if you're not having fun.
—Manuel Gonzales Jr.

My great-grandma, my grandma, Uncle Leo, Aunt Pauline, and my mom returned to Colorado, and Dad stayed in El Paso to recover. It took weeks of healing before he could get out of bed and begin the physical therapy necessary to ease into his new life on one leg. He needed to learn to use his left hand for everything. As soon as he was mobile in a wheelchair, they began to take him outside, and he would be there for hours and hours by himself. I can only imagine what it was like for him to reframe the rest of the life he now had before him. He had to find a new place of meaning, purpose, and identity. He had to rebuild what had been mentally and emotionally broken by his injuries and learn both to live with and to master his new body.

The nurses were kind and would often stop to chat. When the head nurse in charge of his barracks found out Dad liked to build things and loved cars, she brought him a model kit with glue and paint and everything he needed to build it. "Here, try putting this together," she told him. When he did, she brought him an airplane kit. When he finished it, she brought in three more models, and he set to work putting those together.

When he and Uncle Leo were kids, Leo got so good at working with models, he would cut the doors out, install them back in with wires, and you'd be able to open and close them with your fingertips. Then he figured out how to do the same thing with the hood and the trunk. Later models would have those features designed in, but he figured that out before any of those innovations were standard. Dad had learned how to do all this watching his older brother, and as he got more adept at building the models left-handed, he started challenging himself to install these same upgrades.

He always used to tell me, "When you find something hard to do, you don't give up. You keep doing it until you can perfect it."

As he began to get around on crutches by himself, he made his way to the enlisted men's club run by the Red Cross and discovered it had a pool table. At first, it must've seemed ludicrous to think he could play anywhere near how well he'd played before, but at the same time, here was a table no one was using. Why not give it a try? What if he could figure out how to play this game again? Maybe he'd never be as good as he was before, but he could still have fun. His physical skills were different, but he still had his knowledge, wisdom, and understanding of the game and the shots. If he could figure out how to build models single-handed, couldn't he do the same with pool?

So, he racked the balls and picked out a pool cue.

It was like learning the game for the first time again. He knew how to make the shots, but he'd have to teach his body how to shoot them all over again. Since he was shooting with his opposite hand, he had to learn to use his opposite eye to line up his shots instead of his dominant right. He adapted to that pretty quickly. He began by resting the cue stick on the rail and shooting from there. If the cue ball was in the middle of the table, he grabbed the bridge and used that.

He realized that it was not just a matter of switching from one eye to the other, but also switching around the way he pictured the game from right-handed to left. The thought process was similar but mirrored. He slowly began to adapt and reverse things in his mind.

What was harder was that he didn't have enough strength in his left arm to play for very long at a time. His right arm, of course, had been naturally stronger and he'd never used his left as much, so he had to approach the game a little at a time to build up his strength.

He kept at it, and before too long he was playing pretty much every opportunity he got. He said he wasn't very good at first, but the more he played, the more he felt like the game was still there for him. Playing also provided a way to shut out the world and just do something that he remembered from before the war. For brief periods of time, it let him forget everything else and just be himself again.

As simple as it was, it gave him a way of going home that was beyond the plane and bus ride he would soon catch to return to Greeley. It was something the war wasn't able to take away from him.

Pool Therapy

When I was thirteen, I played with my dad in a partners nine-ball pool tournament at The Break in Greeley. As usual, I was the only kid in the tournament. We won with my dad coaching me the whole way through. Just before he passed away, I had a sudden realization that he could have played with anybody in that tournament—there were lots of players stronger than I was who would have loved to play with him. I asked him why he chose me instead when he had so many other options, and he answered, "I wanted to play with who I knew I would have the most fun with."

That was always his attitude. It wasn't about winning; it was about having fun—not that he didn't win a lot anyway and have plenty of fun doing it.

I also know that playing pool was therapeutic for Dad, because I asked him about it one time. While playing, he could zone out the rest of the world. He could forget his injuries, his stresses, his troubles, and just focus on making one shot at a time, lost in eyeballing angles and calculating spins, tinkering with different ways to approach given situations.

It was a game he knew and loved, but it was also a refuge.

When he first got back to Greeley, he'd get lost in play, and they'd have to kick him out when they closed. Games would end late, and he'd want to start a new one right away. On several different occasions, Mom had to come get him, or he probably would have slept on a bench or table somewhere, if they'd have let him.

He didn't just get lost in playing either. He used to study other players to see how they did things, especially the really good players when he got the chance. Two of the best he would hang around with were Gordy Hubert and Adolph Lesser. Gordy was the one who taught him how to use English with the cue ball. Adolph was more stoic and demanded that my dad practice drills to rise to a higher level.

In the initial years back home, I know Dad was still dealing with PTSD, and he'd have high and low points. His injuries were still a sensitive point to him, and if anyone took it easy on him in a game or tried to do something for him uninvited, he'd get upset. In pool, that often focused him to the point where he wouldn't miss a shot. It would help him get "in stroke." Those who knew him well razzed him about it. He'd get into one of those zones with someone, and one of them would joke, "You never should have made him mad," laughing under their breath as he moved from one ball to the next.

I think the teams he formed caught that from him too. One of his good friends, Juan Euresti, once told me about a time my dad was playing in the VNEA International Team Championships in Vegas with him against a French-Canadian team. My dad broke and ran the table against his first opponent. In the third round, when it was my dad's turn to break again, as he pulled out his bridge, the opposing player called over the referee. He claimed that it was illegal for my dad to use a bridge to break. The referee told them it wasn't (probably shaking in disbelief at the question), and Dad broke and ran the table again. But that wasn't the end of it. The rest of the guys on my dad's team took it to heart as well and beat them in three rounds rather than the usual five. It was a drubbing.

When we'd go to Vegas and he'd play a match, I'd always watch how opponents reacted to him the first time they played him. At first it would be like, *Oh, I've got to play this guy?* You could see the mixed emotions on their faces. They'd see him rack the balls, and it was obvious he had done it a thousand times. Then, as soon as my dad made a few balls in a row, you'd see the expression change to concern. You could tell they were thinking, *Oh man, he's for real.* And you could see when they realized they were going to lose that they should have taken him more seriously from the start. But even if they did, most of them still didn't have a chance.

The Shape of a Game

It's always been difficult for me to determine just how much of becoming good at pool is having natural talent and how much is learning the techniques of the game. For most people, you can only teach them so much before they hit a ceiling. I've never really been able to put my finger on it, but I believe there is a feel for the game some have, some develop, and some never realize. There's a way to see the table and shots. There's a rhythm to a pendulum stroke and an eye for shooting. There's a stability and consistency to some people's control of the cue ball that can seem uncanny.

At the same time, there are a lot of simple quirks that can get in the way of any amount of natural ability, so there are certainly skills to be learned to develop more consistent success. Any way you look at it, though, you need to put in what Malcolm Gladwell called the "ten thousand hours" required for mastering any activity, from playing pool to starting a business to applying stucco to constructing a model.

As they say, though, practice doesn't make perfect; it makes permanent. You've got to practice the right way, or all you do is reinforce your quirks.

A good game in which to practice your cue ball control in is nine-ball or ten-ball. Both of these games require you to sink balls sequentially, but don't clutter the table with too many balls to begin with. A good game in which to practice your shots is eight-ball, where you can start off with multiple balls to choose from to create a pattern to the eight ball. Snooker is even better to hone your skills because of the size of the table and the smaller pockets, but snooker tables are far and few between these days. I was lucky that we had one in our home growing up.

Once again, controlling the rock is the goal. Once again, you want to practice always thinking three shots ahead. Where does the ball need to be to give you a good shot on your next ball? Now consider shooting from there to get to the next ball after that. Can you get to where you need to be for your third shot easily from where you'll leave this shot? If not, then consider approaching the next ball from another angle. Does that work better? And then keep working it until you see a pattern for getting shape on your next three shots.

Another thing to practice is forcing yourself to figure out at least three different approaches to sinking the next object ball. This will help you see options for getting shape on the next two balls after. There is always more than just one way to make a shot. In fact, there are usually a handful. Which will be best for setting yourself up for the next two? To be good, you need to master numerous different types of shots, because you never know what you might have to deal with on the table in a given game.

Some setups will feel routine and come to you more naturally than others. Some will sync with the skill set you already have naturally, while others will demand practicing new techniques and iterating on them until you feel like you can rely on them under pressure.

When you play nine- or ten-ball, it forces you to think continually of how you are going to get from the present shot to the next consecutive number—which I believe is the line of thought that separates casual players from enthusiasts. Casual players sink balls as best they can; enthusiasts learn to develop patterns for sinking them in a sequence.

Let the Kids Play

In his book *12 Rules for Life*, Jordan Peterson explains some classic values for being a good human being. Most of them seem a little self-evident once you read them—things like "Stand up straight with your shoulders back," "Make friends with people who want the best for you," and "Set your house in perfect order before you criticize the world." His last two, however, are a little odd. The first is "Do not bother children when they are skateboarding," and the second is "Pet a cat when you encounter one in the street." Not exactly things you might think of as life-altering.

Yet as he digs into them, you see the logic. Skateboarding has many levels, of course, but when you see kids jumping off the top of a set of stairs and trying to land atop the railing down the middle to slide down it as if they were snowboarding and then land gracefully—or not so gracefully—below, it's quite natural to want to shout out, "Don't do that! That looks dangerous! You're going to break a bone!"

Dr. Peterson, however, suggests against this. "Of course it was dangerous," he writes. "Danger is the point. They want to triumph over danger. . . . They weren't trying to be safe. They were trying to become competent—and it's competence that makes people as safe as they can truly be."[15]

While pool doesn't have the same danger element as skateboarding, it does have a competence element. Pool is something that's hard to get good at. It demands trying again and again and often "falling down" by missing shots. It takes some time before you make more shots than you miss in a game, and it takes much longer than that to start clearing a table without missing a shot. It's a frustrating game at times—I mean, it's not golf, but it's still complicated.

But working to master something that is difficult is "as safe as [one] can truly be." Competence breeds confidence, and confidence is very difficult to bottle up in one part of your life versus another. People who are really good at one thing have the natural belief that they can master other areas. It's one of the reasons sports are so important as a training ground for life. Leadership on a football field translates well into leadership in a business environment. They share similar motivational and team-building aspects. Competence teaches you to believe in yourself in all aspects of life.

My dad and my nino (godfather), Uncle Brownie

The last one, of course, is a lot like "take time to stop and smell the flowers." If you see a friendly cat, give it some love. The same goes for dogs, of course. Life is suffering, and we can either contribute to that or help alleviate it. Don't miss a chance to be kind, especially with animals who are so quick to bounce the affection right back. If you're too busy to stop and pet the animals, you're too busy. Plus, cats and dogs are a good safe place to practice kindness. Most of the time they reflect it right back. People are much more complex.

The Art of English

I've saved using spin until this late in the book for a couple of reasons. One, it's not the first thing you need to learn to be good at playing pool. In fact, as odd as it might sound, you can't really get good at using English—learning to put spin on a ball—until you master hitting it straight. If you can't control a straight shot, you can't control a spin shot either.

Another reason is that English is tough to get competent at—but then, like the kids on their skateboards, that's where the thrill of challenge and fun really is.

It's impossible to set up every shot to be straight in, and honestly, you don't really want to. Why? Because getting straight in on your next shot is almost never the best place to be to set yourself up for the ball afterward (the third in your pattern of three). You've got to learn how to work your angles and eventually how to use English. You've got to consider the path you want the cue ball to take to get to the next ball down the line, but if the tangent line won't take the cue ball where you'd like it to go, then you've got to add spin to it to help. It takes some playing time before learning this becomes possible, let alone routine.

So, first things first: Once again, get yourself in position so you are consistent in your shot routine. Learn to aim, understand the tangent line, and learn the geometry of using the rails. Then you'll be ready to begin experimenting with English.

My dad started teaching me English by having me imagine a clock face on the cue ball while standing on the shot line. Anywhere from the center of the cue ball to the center of the top of the cue ball (twelve o' clock) are various degrees of high English. Hitting the cue ball with high English on straight-in shots creates forward spin and causes the cue ball to follow the object ball upon contact. The amount of high English along with the speed of acceleration upon contact is what determines the distance the cue ball will travel after impacting the object ball. Using high English on cut shots causes the cue ball to break off the tangent line away from you. The amount of high English along with the speed of acceleration upon contact is what determines the distance the cue ball will travel along the tangent line, the point at which the cue ball will break off the tangent line, and the distance the cue ball will travel.

An article in the Greeley Tribune *about my family pool heritage*

Dad showed me how there are different ways to hit the cue ball to achieve the same result. For instance, on straight-in shots, hitting the cue ball firm in the center and hitting it soft with extreme high English (twelve o' clock) will each result in the cue ball rolling for a short distance after contact with the object ball.

Anywhere from just below the stun spot to extreme low (six o' clock) on the cue ball, are various degrees of low English also known as draw English. Hitting the cue ball with low English on straight-in shots creates backspin and causes the cue ball to come back toward you after contacting the object ball. Using low English for cut shots causes the cue ball to break off the tangent line toward you after contacting the object ball. The amount of low English along with the speed of acceleration upon contact is what determines the distance the cue ball will travel along the tangent line, the point at which the cue ball will break off the tangent line, and the distance the cue ball will travel.

Just like high English, Dad showed me how there are different ways to hit the cue ball with low English to achieve the same result. For instance, on straight-in shots, hitting the cue ball firm and right below the stun spot and hitting the cue ball soft with extreme low English will both result in the cue ball having slight backspin—coming back toward you for a short distance after contact with the object ball.

After practicing and learning high and low English, he started to teach me how to use right-hand and left-hand English. He taught me that hitting anywhere between the center of the cue ball and the right edge of the cue ball (three o' clock) is right-hand English. Anywhere between the center of the cue ball and left edge of the cue ball (nine o' clock) is called left-hand English. Right English and left English both put sidespin on the cue ball and in most situations are used to change the angle that the cue ball has after contacting the rail. The amount of side English along with the speed of acceleration upon contact is what determines the angle that the cue ball will have after contact with the rail. Depending on the shot, using various degrees of sidespin can create a shallow angle, bring about a larger angle, or even reverse the angle the cue ball has bouncing off the rail.

Learning and understanding how English works in conjunction with the rules of the tangent line is the only way to become an elite player.

With a lot of practice, you will begin to learn how to combine different types of English to advance your control of the cue ball. For example, on any cut shot to your left, hitting the cue ball firm with high right-hand English (two o' clock) will create top and sidespin together and cause the cue ball to follow the tangent line for a few inches, break off the tangent line away from you, and then create a larger angle after contacting the rail.

Learning sidespin is great but comes with its own set of challenges. Anytime you put sidespin on the cue ball, the sidespin is going to cause the cue ball to deflect off the aim-line to the opposite of where you hit the cue ball. For example, when using right-hand English, the cue ball will deflect off the aim line to the left. And vice versa for left-hand English, which will come off to the right. The amount of sidespin along with the speed of acceleration upon contact is what determines the amount of deflection the cue ball will have.

This means that you will need to compensate for the deflection in your shot routine and aim-line. There are many variables when it comes to deflection. The type of cloth on the table, the humidity in the room, the type of pool cue you shoot with, and the type of tip it has all play a role in the amount of deflection. It's important to learn your equipment and the amount of adjustment that's needed when shooting with sidespin.

Then, when playing different tables, like in a tournament, you should shoot a few warmup shots with sidespin to learn quickly how much adjustment is needed for that particular table. If you ever watch professionals warm up at a tournament, you will often see them hitting the cue ball hard with extreme sidespin and missing shots. They are not being careless; they are learning the deflection that happens on that particular table and how much they need to adjust their aim-line.

You see it with the best players, like Shane Van Boening, who I mentioned earlier. Players who get to the top of the game are very, very consistent and are able to control where their balls end up after a shot within about a square inch. They control the cue ball and what happens beyond first contact with the object ball. I know Shane put in hours and hours of practice to get to the top of the game.

Top pool players, like my dad was, have strokes that are incredibly smooth. A lot of people start on smaller tables and can get away with jabby strokes, but the bigger the table and the tighter the pockets, the more the balls have to roll in a straight line, and the more the flaws in your game show up. Top players emphasize follow-through over power. Using the diamonds as measurements, they know how much spin they need—two diamonds' worth? Five diamonds' worth? They know how to hit the cue ball just right for each distance. I'm always amazed when watching great pros like Shane play. It feels like magic, though I know it isn't.

Always Learning

When I was younger and I got good quickly under my dad's training, I played at a really high level all through my teens. At the same time, I remember thinking, *When I really learn how to play this game, I'm going to be pretty deadly.* I knew there was a higher level. I was good, but I always knew I was missing something the pros had that I didn't yet, and I wasn't sure what it was. I knew it was something more than thinking, *The more I play, the better I'll get.* I know there was also some understanding I didn't quite have then that I am developing now, and that's what I'm building my new game around, developing an even deeper and better understanding of the game. That's why I know I can get better than I was then.

At the same time, it makes me laugh when I think how cocky I was. I was already really good, but I'm better now in some ways because now I'm learning to control the cue ball and understand the shape of the game, not just make tough shots. The fun is only starting.

TEN

Be a Teacher

> Whatever you teach makes you better at it, so as soon as you learn something difficult, find someone to teach it to right away.
> —Manuel Gonzales Jr.

As I've looked back over my dad's life and how significant 1968 was, it's hard not to also notice what was happening in the United States at the same time. The Tet Offensive began early that year, and though it was a crushing loss for the Viet Cong and the People's Army, it eventually broke the political will of the United States to keep fighting. Realizing this, just a handful of weeks before Dad's injuries, on March 31, incumbent President Lyndon B. Johnson announced he wouldn't run for reelection.

The next week, on April 4, Martin Luther King Jr. was assassinated.

Robert "Bobby" Kennedy announced his candidacy for the presidency on March 16, just a couple of weeks before LBJ stepped down. While Dad was in the VA hospital, he watched the news of Bobby's victory in the Californian primary on June 5, and then the news of his assassination the next day, the same way he had watched the news of JFK's assassination when he was a teenager. I never spoke with him about those things, but it's hard to imagine that they didn't impact him and how turbulent it must have made that year feel. It was a fateful time in so many ways.

As for Dad, he finally returned to Greeley in November 1968, right around the time that Richard Nixon was elected over Vice President Hubert Humphrey, the first Republican president of the decade. Nixon ran on the promise he would end the war, but the war would limp on until 1972, when the bulk of our troops were finally withdrawn.

I'm sure, though, as Dad returned home, those were the last things he wanted to think about. Despite his previous efforts to dissuade her, Mom was still planning to marry him, and they had a wedding to get ready for.

While Dad was recovering, the two of them wrote back and forth about having a big wedding. Mom's bridesmaids had been selected, and they had the money saved up to cover everything. After Dad got back, though, and they started talking about it, they didn't feel like they really wanted a big wedding anymore. "Why are we going to have a big wedding when we could use the money that we've saved to fix up a house and buy furniture instead?"

So they called off the big bash and opted for a smaller celebration. Instead of worrying through all the details any longer, they started planning for the home they would share. My Grandfather Larry, on my mom's side, had a small piece of land with little houses. One of the houses was off the market because it needed work. Mom and Dad decided to rent it from my grandfather and negotiated a good deal in exchange for fixing it up themselves.

One of Dad's uncles owned a used furniture store in Denver, so they went down and bought couches, beds, a dining room table and chairs, and some rugs for about five hundred dollars of the money they had saved up for the wedding. It was enough furniture for the two bedrooms, the living room, the kitchen, and the bathroom in what they had started calling their "little casita."

Then they set about fixing it up. The ceiling had collapsed, so Dad replaced it. They painted, and they got everything in working order. By the time of the wedding, they had their little casita in good enough shape to host their reception.

They married at Lady of Our Peace Church in Greeley on December 14, 1968. Mom's Grandma Griego, my Grandma Mary, my Grandma Esther (Mom's mom), and my Aunt Mary Helen supervised the cooking. It was a full celebration with music, dancing, and the specialties of all the matriarchs of the family.

The big day

The newlyweds

Ready to start their new life together

By 9 or 10 p.m., Mom and Dad were ready for everyone to go home, but Uncle Tommy, his brothers, and their dad were just getting warmed up. They were there until 4 a.m., when my mom finally asked, "Aren't you going to go home?" With that, they decided to let the new couple have their house to themselves. Mom and Dad were so tired, they went straight to bed and did all the cleanup the next day.

Finally, roughly a year after their engagement, they were ready to start their lives together.

Learning Is a Group Activity

One of the things I saw Dad do time and again was teach something he had just learned. I remember when he would get back from learning something new from his VCR-fixing friend in Denver, he would try to teach it to my sister Renee or me. Renee became his full-time student and began to love working on VCRs with him. She got really good at it. She was the second worker in his shop with him for years.

He was always the same with anyone who showed any interest in something he did. He'd stop right in the middle of a game sometimes to teach someone watching how to make the shot he'd just sunk when they asked about it. I think people enjoyed gathering around him to watch him play, but I'll bet there were often as many people, if not more, who gathered around hoping for an impromptu lesson on a shot they didn't even know existed before they came in that day.

My dad seemed to have radar for someone he could learn from and a similar radar for those open to learning. Whether it was watching VHS tapes of pool-playing professionals or when someone really good came through one of the pool halls, he'd watch them closely to see if they did anything he hadn't seen before. If he noticed something that was unique about their stance, their stroke, the way they lined up on the balls, or whatever it might be, he'd ask about it. I think every top player in Colorado and well-known professional contributed to his game in some way over the years, and once he learned something, then he'd go teach it to someone else to be sure he understood it and had the technique down. In fact, my son, MG4, once told me he'd never met a top player in Colorado who didn't have a story about learning something from his grandfather.

If he didn't have anyone else to teach, Dad always had me, and then there were the guys he'd gathered into teams for tournaments. When I was thirteen, my dad introduced me to another teen pool player from our hometown of Greeley named James Hilzer, who was a year older and eventually became a best friend. He and I practiced together a lot in our basement. As we grew in the game together, we began to travel to Denver just about every weekend to challenge anyone we could find. As pool-playing partners, we found out that we were in sync, we were tough to beat, and it was a great way to make money.

James credits my dad with helping him become one of Colorado's best. James has won countless local tournaments, state tournaments, regional tournaments, and also the VNEA International Championship Open Singles nine-ball tournament in 1995. Although my dad taught and shared knowledge with numerous people, the only other person I know whom Dad taught as closely and as often as

BE A TEACHER

James and me is my oldest son, Manuel IV, who also had an international championship win in the 2021 VNEA Intermediate Team Tournament.

Dad had a dozen or so friends I would also consider his "students": Victor Vargas, Ray Lopez, Jaime Lechuga, Aaron Westcott, just to name a few. They would get together at the local pool hall or come to the house, and my dad would teach them. Watching him teach, I always learned something new myself.

He also taught a lot of people randomly as the opportunity presented itself. He seemed to be able to teach each person something to help them improve their game according to the level they were at. One person he would help improve their stance, show how to get a better line on a ball, or help them remember to follow through. Another he would teach different ways to use English. Another he would teach a diamond system for doing kicks and banks. I'm sure he taught something to a couple hundred different people over the years. Maybe even more. He was willing to pass on his wisdom to anyone who crossed his path and acted interested in the game. It was just part of the way he respected and served other people.

My oldest son, Manuel VI, used to love to go over to his grandpa's on Sundays two or three hours before the regular tournaments they had at Match Ups in Fort Collins. His grandpa would walk him through different drills before he would let him hit a rack of balls. One week they would work on drawing the cue ball, the next would be high English shots, and so on.

Dad also always had a way of mixing pool-playing tips with life advice. Baldemar Gonzalez told me that one time he was practicing long rail shots, which he had trouble with, and Dad, who was in a wheelchair at the time, rolled over and asked, "Do you need help with that shot?"

"Yeah," he said, "if you have time."

Dad looked at him and said, "All I have left in life is time."

He helped Baldemar a good deal with his pool game that day but also with his outlook on life. Baldemar said he learned from my dad not to take the little things for granted and always to give his best effort.

Dad was always free with advice, and many of the top players in Colorado conferred with him if he was around when they were playing. Damon Lemoine, who became a top player in Colorado, would always go to Dad if he made a mistake and ask what he could have done better. He remembered several times when Dad found him in Las Vegas just to ask how things were going and where he was in his bracket. Friendship is a two-way street, and many considered Dad to be a good friend.

Another guy who used to play at the Break with us a lot, Dominic Brown, grew up to love pool from watching my dad play. My mom used to babysit him and his brother and sister, and he'd watch Dad practicing on our snooker table. He said he was always afraid to ask to play on it because it was so beautiful. Dad was so good, he said, but what stuck with him was Dad's humility. He was always surprised he was willing to take time out to teach him a shot.

Tim Cole, another of Dad's friends and students, remembers a time at Shakespeare's in Denver when he was in a tight nine-ball match and Dad pulled him aside and gave him some advice. Dad reminded Tim that not every turn at the table has to be a table run. It's okay, and even very smart, to play safe and be patient. After that, he never lost another game in that match. "I learned something from Manny every time we talked," he wrote to me after Dad passed, "and he told me so many stories. He had me laughing so hard at times it felt like my ribs were broke and had me crying. . . . I think he had that effect on everyone, and we were all better off having met Manny and knowing him in each of our ways."

The Carom Shot

Sometimes when guys feel they don't have a shot, they will play defense, a "safety," leaving the cue ball in a place they feel you won't have a shot either, trying to force you to open the table so they have a better chance of sinking a ball their next turn. Although a safety can be a smart strategic shot, I'm pretty sure my dad always thought there was an offensive shot, even when no one else could see it.

One time a guy tried to play defense on my dad, but because Dad had played so much snooker, he saw a shot that no one else in the room even knew existed.

The balls were still pretty tightly clumped after the break, and the guy had hit his object ball and sent the cue ball into the area between the stack of balls and the back rail. To most players, there was no offensive shot available. But Dad knew that if he shot his object ball off the back of the stack at just the right spot, it would send the object ball directly into the corner pocket while the rest of the balls would scatter. Sure enough, he hit it just perfect, sank his object ball, and the rest scattered. From there, he had a whole new table to shoot at. It was a time when experience really kicked in for him. He saw a way where no one else did. It was a shot he'd never have even dreamed of trying had he not played it before.

The shot he took is called a "carom" shot: striking your object ball and ricocheting it off another ball to send the object ball to the pocket. In this case, he shot the object ball into the stack of balls, where it hit one ball, ricocheted it off another ball in the stack, and that angled the object ball into the corner pocket. He made the shot, breaking up the cluster, and now he had several options for where to shoot next.

Dad taught me how to get the most out of a shot when sending the cue ball into the stack. One year, I was playing in the VNEA International Team Tournament against Canada. Going into my game, Canada only needed two points to beat us, which meant the only chance for us to win the match was if I ran the table before they sank two balls. Unfortunately, the break was to them, so they thought they'd play clever. Their strategy to win was to try what's called a "safety break." My opponent hit the ball softly so that only four balls contacted the rails and the balls in the stack stayed mostly together. With the balls clustered, they thought, I would have to break them apart, and then it should've been easy for their guy to make two balls and win the round.

Instead, I looked at the table, and my immediate thought was, *Wow, there's the same shot my dad just taught me.*

My instinct for this shot was to use English toward the stack, thinking that would spin the ball into the cluster so that it would scatter the balls even more, but Dad had told me, "If you do that, you're liable to get the cue ball stuck in the middle of all the other balls and only have tight shots, if any shot at all. Instead, use English to spin it away from the stack after you hit it, and then your cue ball won't get caught up in the stack, and you'll have a better selection from there."

Had he not told me that, I bet I would have been in a real fix and the Canadians' strategy probably would have worked. The thing is, though, he *had* told me.

Never try to outfox a fox.

I set up the shot and lined up the tip of my pool cue for "inside" English to give the cue ball spin to kick out after it hit the stack. The breakout shot worked perfectly, the balls scattered, and the cue ball spun away from the others and found a place to rest that gave me some good options. I think I was just as surprised as anyone in the room that it had worked so well.

I found the eight, worked my way back from it to see a pattern for running the table, and then lined up the first shot of the series.

I think it was the most satisfying time I ever ran a table in my life.

Overcoming Resistance to Growth

In her book, *Finding Your Nxt*, Cindy Carrillo says the number-one reason people don't grow or fail to live their lives fully is fear of the unknown. As we discussed before, what you don't know *can* hurt you, and this may be one of the biggest ways. Fear discourages us from living our best life before we even begin to pursue it. What we don't know seems so large that change for the better feels impossible.[16]

Steven Pressfield goes so far as to personify that fear—what he calls "Resistance"—as a shadowy force that works to keep us from our dreams, from our artistic endeavors, or from our life calling. In *The War of Art*, he writes,

Every sun casts a shadow, and genius's shadow is Resistance. As powerful as our soul's call to realization, so potent are the forces of resistance arrayed against us. Resistance is faster than a speeding bullet, more powerful than a locomotive, harder to kick than crack cocaine. . . .

Resistance defeats us. If tomorrow morning by some stroke of magic every dazed and benighted soul woke up with the power to take the first step towards pursuing his or her dreams, every shrink in the directory would be out of business. Prisons would stand empty. The alcohol and tobacco industries would collapse, along with the junk food, cosmetic surgery, and infotainment business, not to mention pharmaceutical companies, hospitals, and the medical profession from top to bottom. Domestic abuse would become extinct, as would addiction, obesity, migraine headaches, road rage, and dandruff.[17]

In our information age, fearing the unknown may seem a little silly, since we have a whole world of information at our fingertips through a simple internet search, but too much information can be worse than not enough. Even worse, of course, is when most of what is available to us is either wrong or contradicts other information. In such cases, the more we learn, the more confused we become. Not exactly helpful. Resistance wins again.

You've got to have a reliable source.

I think this is one of the reasons communities are so important: they are safe and dependable places to learn. And I don't mean schools, though they are a kind of community. I mean the places we frequent in daily life—our workplaces, the corner café, sporting events, the local bar, and of course, the pool hall, at least if someone like my dad is turning it into a network of friends and family rather than just someplace to go and hang out and drink beer.

Community doesn't just mean showing up. It demands participation, and it depends on people who are connectors to facilitate that participation.

I'm not sure if you know, but America is experiencing a loneliness epidemic that very few are talking about and is as deadly as smoking. We are more disconnected than we have ever been, and it feels like our connecting skills are worse than ever, which I'm not sure is a result of that epidemic or the cause of it. Science is only now discovering how important human connection is. As US Surgeon General Vivek Murthy found in traveling the country and talking to people about health concerns, loneliness wasn't a frontline complaint. It wasn't even identified directly as a health ailment. Loneliness ran like a dark thread through many of the more obvious issues that people brought to my attention, like addiction, violence, anxiety, and depression. The teachers and school administrators and many parents I encountered, for example, voiced a growing concern that our children were becoming isolated—even, or perhaps especially, those who spent much of their time in front of their digital devices and on social media.[18]

One of the things I feel Dad did in creating community was give people a safe place to take on the unknown, both in pool and in life. He built a community by being willing to teach, and that was contagious. He gave people a safe place to try and fail safely a few times before finding success. (I might add that Ms. Carrillo's number-two reason for resisting change is "fear of failure.") Dad helped people find a place of competence. A place where making mistakes was okay and part of the learning and growing process.

Within the community of friends and family Dad helped knit together, you could find good information because people were trying to be sincerely helpful. Because Dad shared freely, others did the same. It gave people a place for their questions and concerns to be heard. It taught people how to love one another in very practical ways.

Wherever You Are Is the Perfect Place to Start

Sometimes players have bad habits they've created over years of bad form, and it can be tricky helping them improve. Rather than insisting on perfect form, for some people it's better to work with how they are compensating because of improper form—at least at first—rather than trying to send them back to zero and starting over. What they have been doing up to this point has somewhat worked for them, and there is often a smaller tweak in their practice that can bring them more success rather than throwing their entire sense of the game off and relearning from scratch.

It also depends on what they are after. If they want the chance to go pro someday, then rebuilding from the beginning is best, but if they are just looking to get better without hours and hours (and hours) of practice, changing a few smaller things will get them to their goal faster, and they can start making more shots sooner rather than later. If their goal is simply to play better and have more fun, then making tweaks can be easier and help them have more fun right away.

Dad would usually start by asking them what they saw the cue ball do when they were asking why they missed a shot. If the object ball doesn't do what you want it to, it's because the cue ball didn't do what you wanted it to do first, and that's because, for some reason, you didn't strike it in the way you thought you did.

Generally, you can get to the same spot on the table with at least two different types of English. There are a lot of times when straight stun and following that ninety-degree tangent angle off the object ball will get you to the center of the table. But you can also use a little bit of high right English, and then once the cue ball hits the rail, it'll come off and you'll get to the exact same spot. Helping people understand those different approaches gives them a small thing they can start to experiment with, and as they become more successful, they feel a sense of competence, which makes the game more fun.

There was one guy who had been playing for about twenty years and never seemed to get any better than being a C player. He asked my dad for some tips. Dad started teaching him about English and how an adjustment is needed in your aim line because the cue ball deflects off the aim line with right and left English. It seemed okay when he tried to put right English on the ball, but when he tried to add left English, he would lose his accuracy. My dad watched that a couple of times, and then he set up an object ball on the center diamond of the end rail, put the cue ball on the spot, and told him, "Aim to hit the object ball straight on, but with one tip of left English."

He got down and aimed for what he thought was the center of the object ball.

"Okay, freeze," my dad said. He took a half step to the right. "You're aiming over here."

"No, I'm not."

"Yes, you are," my dad said. "Look at where the back end of your cue stick is."

He looked and saw that his cue stick wasn't straight but angled off to the side slightly.

Dad laid his pool cue on the table in a straight line from where he was aiming to show him the line. "You naturally adjust for the English you put on the ball every time you shoot. You've learned over the years to compensate for that."

He looked and realized my dad was right. "Oh, wow," he said. "I never noticed that."

After realizing what he was doing, he finally understood how he was naturally adjusting his aim without even knowing it. With this newfound knowledge he began to understand that shot after shot, his aim line was not actually where he thought it was. It was causing inconsistencies in his shot-making, especially when using English. Dad had opened his eyes to see exactly where he was aiming with or without English, which allowed him to adjust for deflection when needed. This resulted in more consistent shot-making and better cue ball control.

It's tough to overestimate how huge a small, new understanding can be. It gave him the ability to correct the way he naturally aimed and overcome habits that had been preventing him from getting better. My dad gave him a solid foundation to build on that would allow for him to grow in the game that he had loved playing for all those years.

It's good to stay small with casual advice; otherwise, it can be discouraging. You've got to meet people where they are. Big changes can take the fun out of the game for a casual player, and sometimes they will stop playing rather than put in the practice demanded by larger changes. With the right advice, it's possible to move them gradually in the right direction. When they see the improvement, they'll stay motivated to improve even more, and the game stays fun all along the way.

ELEVEN

Live Gracefully

> Bullets aren't so bad. It's the stuff that goes "*Boom!*" you should worry about.
> —Manuel Gonzales Jr.

Dad had a way of never getting caught up when others were acting like the sky was going to fall or making a big thing out of a disagreement or slight. It was hard to "ruffle his feathers." I think it's one of the things that made him a great referee, a great team captain, and a great tournament director. It was Kevin Silverberg who told me that my dad once said: "Bullets aren't so bad. It's the stuff that goes '*Boom!*' you should worry about." I know he was making light of his own trauma. Over the years, he'd seen plenty of fellow soldiers come back with bullet wounds who had little more than scars to show for the injuries. Relatively speaking, that was pretty minor compared to the things that went "*Boom!*" like getting hit with an RPG.

In his own wry way, I think he was saying that life had thrown its worst at him, and he had survived and gone on to live a full life. You could take a few bullets and recover without much sign of them. You could overcome those injuries if they didn't kill you. There was no reason to let those scars get you down. There was a lot worse out there in life that you could survive as well, but those things weren't going to leave you the same afterward. Worry about those bigger things, and definitely don't let anything else push your buttons or make you lose control. People are too important to get upset with over little things. And honestly, there are very few things that aren't, relatively speaking, little.

Early Married Life

Mom told me she continued to work at the hospital after they got married, cleaning rooms and making ninety cents an hour. That doesn't seem like much now, but her dad had told her she'd have to go work in the beet fields if she wasn't in school, but she landed the hospital gig instead. She had worked there since she dropped out of ninth grade. Dad wanted her to quit, but without him having anything steady, she felt like she shouldn't. Mom was driving a green GTO back then, and Dad had learned to drive it. He'd drop her off and go hang out with friends.

Dad didn't go back to playing pool right away when he got back to Greeley. It was a year or so before he picked up a pool cue again. He was still getting some support money from the VA at the time. He never talked about having a hard time adjusting to being back in the States, but I'm sure there were issues that kept him from wanting to take orders from anyone else again anytime soon. He was mostly his own boss as far back as I can remember.

Mom and Dad

Mom was making about three hundred dollars a month, and part of that was going to her car payments. What Dad was getting in benefits was enough to make ends meet, but just barely. They were getting by but still managed to save up enough to make a down payment on a new house on Twelfth Avenue and Sixth Street in Greeley sometime during the summer of 1969. They bought it for seven thousand dollars. My older sister, Denise, was born the following September, not very long before they moved in.

It was Mom's midwife who told them about the house as they were preparing for Denise's birth. The house belonged to an older woman who was moving into a nursing home, and she wanted to sell her place quickly. They visited it, loved it, and made an offer.

Those early years were tough as Dad was working through the aftermath of his experience in Vietnam. He had horrible nightmares and would wake up screaming in the middle of the night. He and Mom would get up and go into the living room and pray together until he re-collected himself. Mom often went back to bed since she had to work the next day, but Dad would sometimes stay up later and then sleep late into the next day because of his episodes.

Left to right: Dad, Mom, me, Denise, and Renee

Dad had to adapt to a lot of things, both physically and emotionally, being back in the United States, but he wasn't slow to jump in to help others. I believe it was one of the only things he did that made him feel alive. He would help Mom carry groceries from the car and even learned how to change cloth diapers one-handed. They were always a little loose, Mom once told me, but they were good enough with the safety pins snapped and everything. He did that for all three of us kids in the years to follow. My sister Renee was born in 1972, and I came along about five years later, in 1977.

Dad, Renee (standing), and Denise, before I came on the scene

Dad needed to find a new purpose and mission in life after the war. He loved his family, but that didn't keep him busy enough, and when he wasn't focused on a task, his memories would haunt him. He still loved to work on cars, so he decided to go back to school to get an associate's degree in automobile mechanics. To qualify to go to college, he first needed to get his GED, so he audited courses in the Greeley School District until he felt ready for the exam. He took it and passed. It was a first step in regaining control of his life.

Left to right: Denise, Renee, me, Mom, and Dad (I was always in the middle!)

Once he had that degree, he went to the VA for counseling and testing for further rehabilitation.

He told them he wanted to be a mechanic, but they tried to temper his dreams and told him he should learn to be a bookkeeper instead. He took some courses at the University of Northern Colorado in bookkeeping and even got a bookkeeping job, but he didn't enjoy it at all. He eventually left the job, and against the advice of the VA counselors, he enrolled in Aims Community College and took auto mechanics courses.

One of the VA counselors, John Reale, was assigned to him and followed his progress. As Dad kept succeeding, John helped find money to work with him to create special tools he could use in his work as a mechanic. Dad did a lot of the design for these tools himself, constantly tinkering to get them just right.

One of them was a power impact wrench that attached to his amputated arm through a prosthetic. Reale once told a reporter, "Manny and I spent hours together working on those tools, some three-hundred-plus altogether, and then we would get together with the builder and test out the ideas."[19] The prosthetic had an insulated fiberglass fitting that would help prevent him from being shocked. The wrench was air-driven and powered by a compressor. With Reale, Dad also designed a special prosthetic leg to replace his crutch while he worked. This allowed him to stand more naturally over the engine wells, but I don't think he ever really used it much. At least I never saw him wear it.

Dad working on an engine

Dad graduated from Aims in 1974 with an associate's degree of applied science in automobile mechanics. I know Dad wanted to go into business for himself and open an auto shop at the time, so he went back to school after that to get a second degree in business administration. His efforts were noticed a couple of times by the *Greeley Tribune*, who published two or three local interest stories about him.

For the most part, Mom and Dad were both homebodies and lived for us kids. Neither of them liked to drink much, and Mom would go out dancing with her girlfriends every once in a while, but that was about it. They liked to be together at home, fixing things up.

More than anything, Mom was there for Dad. On more than one occasion, I know he told people that if it weren't for her, he wasn't sure what he would have done. A lot of men coming back from Vietnam were less injured than Dad was physically, but they seemed to suffer far more emotional trauma because they didn't have anyone there for them. From the very beginning of their marriage, they knew they were soul mates, and they stuck close to each other. They hadn't been married long before they were completing each other's sentences. They always seemed to know what the other was thinking, even when I was a kid. In other words, yeah, I couldn't get away with anything.

Mom and Dad

Mom and Dad again—I couldn't leave either of these out!

Mom and Dad were very active with us growing up. We went camping together. Dad would play baseball with us, even batting with one hand and running bases with his crutches. He'd jump on the trampoline with us, one time breaking a finger because he got too into trying to do tricks.

I remember sitting with Dad and handing him tools as he worked on those cars. Whatever we were doing, when he could, he liked to have at least one of us kids around. If Dad was working on a particularly cool old car, we'd pack up a cooler with drinks and food and all ride together in the car to the drive-in theater.

Dad had a few different jobs while I was growing up, but mostly when I was younger. One of the things he really enjoyed was working at the information desk for the VA helping people learn about the benefits available to them. He also had a job for a while at Pars Auto Parts and a position at Gifford and Western Gravel Company weighing the trucks. I think when Uncle Leo suggested they open a video rental store together, he found something he could do well that would allow him to be with his family more. All three of us kids worked there with him, and I think he loved that. I know I sure enjoyed being there with him.

The Massé Shot

When my dad first taught me how to hit a massé shot, we were on a nine-foot table in our house, and he had just described how I needed to elevate my cue stick to hit down on the ball to create sidespin, and he showed me exactly where to hit it. The first time I tried it, it curved around a couple of balls and sank the object ball. A whole new world opened up to me. I got really excited.

Dad said, half laughing, "You like that, huh?"

I had to admit, "Yeah, I did."

The massé shot is the most difficult shot to be accurate with in pool. To get the extreme spin you need, you hit straight down on the ball as if you were giving it English from above to make it slide out in one direction but then have so much spin that, when it stops sliding, the spin takes over and brings it back in the other direction. It creates a half arc in the ball and is very useful if you're shooting at an object ball with other balls directly in the path to it. Once you see someone hit one successfully for the first time, you'll know just how much more pool there is to master.

A lot of pool halls forbid even trying massé shots, because, since it demands such a hard downward stroke on the ball, it's easy to damage and tear the cloth on a table if you're not very practiced at it. It's also a shot you will hardly ever need because you usually have better options. You could use a rail or two (or three) or even go for a carom shot. There will, however, be shots now and again where the extreme spin of a massé is your best option, so it's good to know what it is and have practiced it enough to have a good feel for it. Until you do, you can use something from the rest of the repertoire.

Think of it like any other spin shot except that you're hitting down through the ball instead of hitting the ball on a side. If you think of the small clock face on the surface of the ball that we talked about a couple of chapters ago, you're going to do the same thing here, but this time imagine it on the top of the ball as you look down on it from above. If you want extreme backspin, you'll shoot at six o'clock. If you want the ball to move right and then spin back to the left, then you hit the ball on the left or at nine o'clock, or at three o'clock if you want it to kick left and then come back right.

The trick, of course, is that unlike a straight shot where pretty much any magnitude, hard or soft, will take the cue ball on a line to impact the object ball, there is only one magnitude that will take your cue ball along the correct curve to hit the object ball. Too little force will spin the ball wide, and too much will spin the ball too tightly. It's easy to end up missing the object ball altogether. Hitting exactly the right spot on the object ball is even trickier. You have to have an incredible feel for the power needed. Plus, you need to be able to strike down hard on the cue ball but be able to stop before your cue tip hits the table and does damage.

So, it's good to know what a massé shot is but not use it on anyone else's table until you're very practiced at it. Then when you do practice it, you should be under the careful instruction of a player who knows the shot well. Lucky for me, I had just such a great teacher. In order to shoot a massé shot, my dad would have to put his custom bridge on its side to gain the height needed. It was a shot that he practiced enough to become consistent at it. He used it to get out of "safeties" played by his opponent when other options were not available. I can remember the look of amazement and frustration on his opponents' faces when he would pull it off. They were amazed that he could do it but also frustrated, thinking they had him "locked up," not knowing he had the key.

Dad shooting a jump shot

Another way that he would get out of a good safety was with a jump shot. I'm not talking about scooping underneath the cue ball to make it hop over the ball in front of it, which is illegal in today's game, and another good way to tear the cloth. A legal jump shot requires that you hit the cue ball from above at an angle that forces the cue ball to bounce off the table's slate and hop over the ball in front of it. The basics behind a proper jump shot include elevating your cue to the same angle that you want the cue ball to have while bouncing off the slate. From this perspective, you have a new "center ball," and that is where you need to make contact.

To do this, my dad would again put his bridge standing on its side so that he could have a sharp angle to execute the jump shot. As he did with every other shot, he practiced it enough to be consistent at it so he could get out of typical safeties. To see a man with one arm and one leg even attempting this is unbelievable, much less watching him have success doing it. Simply amazing!

The Habit of Perspective

In his book *Don't Sweat the Small Stuff . . . And It's All Small Stuff*, author Richard Carlson writes,

> Whenever we're dealing with bad news, a difficult person, or a disappointment of some kind, most of us get into certain habits, ways of reacting to life—particularly adversity—that don't serve us very well. We overreact, blow things out of proportion, hold on too tightly, and focus on the negative aspects of life. . . .
>
> Happily, there is another way to relate to life—a softer, more graceful path that

makes life seem easier and the people in it more compatible. This "other way" of living involves replacing old habits of "reaction" with new habits of perspective. These habits enable us to have richer, more satisfying lives.[20]

I have to say, Dad had that habit of perspective.

First, he knew who he was and who he wasn't. I think it's hard to get offended if you know who you are, because when someone who doesn't know you strikes out at you (or, more often, I think, doesn't know themselves), their words don't really carry any weight. They can't hurt you. Dad knew nothing anyone in a tournament ever did was going to be close to what he had experienced before, so deep down in his soul he knew that anything negative they threw at him was more about their insecurities than his own. Knowing that allowed him to meet them where they were and figure out the best way forward from there. More often than not, they ended up thanking him for it.

Another element of perspective was that Dad focused on helping others and lifting them up as best he could. He had nothing to prove, and if he did, he would rather do it with a screwdriver or pool cue in his hand. I think he felt his highest calling playing pool was to create community, even more than becoming a great champion himself. He was kind and he listened, because he genuinely wanted to get to the heart of what others were saying. If he didn't hear them, he couldn't help them.

That didn't mean he always wanted to make them happy, but he wanted to help them grow and learn the rules and why the rules are the way they are. Really, in pool, the rules are practical, but they are also about etiquette—how people should behave and how people should respect one another. There was a decorum when he played that others found hard to escape, and he established it first and foremost by setting a proper example.

Dad also understood human beings and our tendency to make mistakes and then feel guilty about them—so guilty sometimes we'd try to deny them. We often talk about a dancer being graceful as she moves across a floor; Dad was graceful like that as he played pool, but also graceful—as in "full of grace"—when it came to dealing with others. He didn't have a short fuse. He had so much self-respect that it was impossible for others to disrespect him. He was patient and took the time to help them figure out what they really needed, which wasn't always what they thought they wanted. And he always seemed to have a quip for lightening the mood or defusing tension with a laugh.

Pool Is a Game of Mastery

Pool is a game of mastery that you can never really master. It's situational, like chess or poker, but it also demands skill, like baseball; it is an individual sport where you're all on your own, like tennis; and it demands the understanding of a physics professor, the knowledge of a geometry teacher, and the prowess of a bookie to calculate the right shot. It also demands incredible self-awareness and honesty in understanding one's own limitations and abilities—as well as that of the table and balls—and the courage to be constantly trying new things and seeking new and better players to take on.

To let the game define you is a recipe for frustration. If you define your ability by shots missed or miscalculated, the game will always beat you. Instead, you must have a mindset that focuses on getting better and enjoy the journey, shot by shot. You must savor the challenges given to you in each new game. Let the focus it demands be your meditation—your prayer even. Let the computations for setting up the shot be a game in and of itself. Enjoy the process and learn as much as you can along the way.

And definitely keep things in perspective. Live with grace, have grace for others, and have grace for yourself. That's where the richness is, and that's where the fun is. If you can find the way to do that in how you work, play, socialize, and stay healthy, you'll be all the better for it.

TWELVE

Never Give Up

> You're not beaten until the last ball drops. The game isn't won by the person who makes the best shot but by the person who makes the last shot.
> —Manuel Gonzales Jr.

A little over a year before I was born, Dad had a match that was featured in the local paper. I don't know if he'd played any tournaments before then—it was in 1976, nine years after he came home from Vietnam—but I think it was the first time he was recognized as one of the best players in northern Colorado.

Once he was back and had started playing again, he said it took about a year before he felt he was returning to the form he had before he got on that bus to Fort Campbell in 1967. Gordy Hubert, who played mostly at Dutch's in Greeley, and Adolph Lesser, who was considered the one to beat at Sportsman's in Eaton, were the best players in the area at the time. As I mentioned before, both of them taught my dad a great deal. Adolph was also

CONTROL THE ROCK

well-known because he had played legend Willie Mosconi in an exhibition match years before and was the leader of a local polka band.

Dad, of course, became friends with both of them and considered them his mentors. There were no better players, no more consistent tournament winners, in all of northern Colorado than these two.

To get a bit of publicity for the Pool Palace, its owner, Jack Maher, sponsored an invitational competition between two local pool players. A hundred-dollar donation and all gate receipts would go to the Cancer Crusade in the name of the winner. He invited Dad and Adolph Lesser to compete in the event.

The match was held on a Tuesday night, and a crowd of about sixty-five gathered to watch. The game was snooker, which is scored rather than decided by a winning ball. Snooker is played with fifteen red balls, each worth one point, six numbered balls of different colors that are all worth more points, and of course a cue ball. Of the colored number balls, yellow is worth two points, green is three, brown four, blue five, pink six, and black seven. The goal is to sink, or "pot," the most points.

The rules are that you have to sink a red ball at the start of any turn; then you can shoot any colored number ball you would like. The red ball stays down in the pocket, and the colored number ball is then re-spotted in its designated position. You then shoot another red ball, and so on, until you miss or commit a foul and lose your turn. After all the red balls are made, the remaining colored number balls have to be shot in order of their value—two through seven—and this time, they don't get re-spotted. The game ends when either all the colored number balls have been sunk or there are not enough points left on the table for the losing player to retake the lead.

In the first game, Dad won 45–30, but Adolph came back to win the second, 43–33. In the third and match-deciding game, after all the reds had been pocketed, Dad ran the green and brown balls scoring nine points and going up 37–12, leaving only 18 points left on the table—not enough for Adolph to come back.

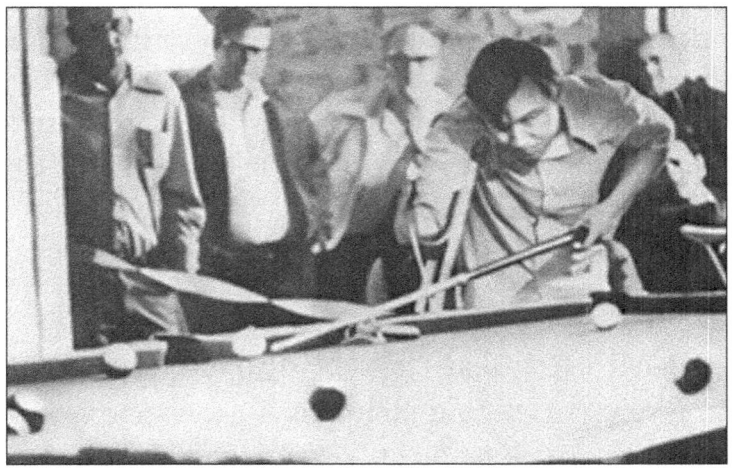

From the Greeley Tribune *article on the exhibition match with Adolph Lesser*

Adolph walked up and laid his cue stick on the table, shaking Dad's left hand with his right. The match was over.

Dad had beaten his teacher. As far as I know, that was the first of many championships Dad competed in and won. He was now among the best players in Colorado. He organized teams to win local, national, and international tournaments and would eventually be named to the VNEA Hall of Fame. Being selected into the VNEA Hall of fame was well deserved and probably his greatest accomplishment in his pool-playing career. It recognized everything he put into the pool community, including being a great player, coach, teacher, referee, tournament director, and role model of the game. His induction celebration was one of the best times our family has ever experienced.

What he accomplished over his career still amazes me as well as everyone who had the pleasure to know him.

Never Say Die

In some games, like football, basketball, or soccer, there's a time limit. As a game gets closer to the clock ticking down to zero, who will win has a lot to do with what the score is and how many opportunities are left for the team that is behind to score. When the clock stops, the game is over. Some games, however, are decided long before that if one team builds up too great a lead. Playing out the rest of the game can be a foregone conclusion, and fans tend to start thinking of getting a head start out of the parking lot.

But pool is a game with no time limit, like baseball and tennis. No matter how far behind you are, if you can string the right number of successes together, the other team has to stick around to watch you beat them. There's no milking the clock or taking a knee. The game continues until the winning shot, winning point, last out, or walk-off hit is made.

Because of this, for the most part, timed games are about the past. Sometimes games are over by halftime—sometimes even by the end of the first quarter. This, of course, has a lot to do with the attitude of the team that is trailing. Sometimes they can come back if they don't defeat themselves by giving in, but not always. Comebacks are rare, which is why they are so great to watch. When a game is close, it can be all about who scored last and how much time is left when they did. You end up getting beat by the clock almost as much as by the other team.

In games like pool, baseball, tennis, etc., it's really about the future. What has happened doesn't matter as much as what you can make happen next. The past is important, but if you can line up enough "nexts," you can come back and win, and there's nothing like running a table when you're coming from way behind.

In pool, unlike baseball and tennis, the other player can't do anything to stop you from stringing together successes either (other than, of course, the mental intimidation games some players try to play). In baseball, they could make a great defensive play, and in tennis, they could win the exchange of shots instead of you, but in pool, it's all in your hands. You can keep going as long as you keep making shots. Only missing or scratching will stop you and give your opponent the chance to retake the table.

Dad at another tournament in Las Vegas

And it's not just about what happens in the future—it's about what *you* make happen in the future: how you approach it, how confidently and courageously you face it, and how accurately you apply your skill. Because of this, no lead is insurmountable. You're never beaten until the deciding ball drops. To be down 25–10 with a minute left in a football game is to be beaten, except in the rarest of instances. To be down 25–10 in a game of snooker is just another point in the game. It all depends on what happens next.

Because of this, you have to keep your head up and have a hopeful attitude, because winning the mental game is just as important in pool as in any other game. Just like when Dad told me I was playing the table rather than any opponent out there, you have to keep from letting your thought pattern beat you. It can be really hard to get a missed shot out of your head, even one you missed three games ago. But the past is the past, and when you're playing pool, it has no binding relationship to your next shot. It should take up no space in your mind. It's one of the things that should go when you "clear the mechanism." It's all about what you do in the present to sink the next ball in sequence to clearing the table and sinking the winning ball (or amassing an insurmountable lead).

If we were playing first to win seven games and you'd lost six games, you aren't beat yet. If your opponent won six in a row, so can you. I know that's true, because I was down 0–6 one time and ended up beating the guy seven games in a row to win. The whole time I was chewing on what Dad had told me about nothing being settled until the last shot. I shut everything else out and played the table, picturing my three shots at a time, and my streak of successful shots came together. I found a way. It didn't hurt that my dad was watching the match either. I always felt like I could do anything when he was around.

A lot of tournaments are double elimination, so even losing a match isn't losing in those tournaments, until you've lost twice. You just can't let yourself give up. Truthfully, you are the only one who can beat you.

I remember going to a huge VNEA Tournament in Las Vegas with something like five hundred players in it. I lost my very first match, but it was double elimination. I doubled down through the loser's bracket, which basically meant I played one match after another, all day and evening long, until I could get back to play in the finals bracket. I ended up taking fifth, which I was pretty proud of in a field like that.

I also remember one winter when Dad was playing in a tournament in Casper, Wyoming, getting ready to play a race-to-four-games match, and he turned around to find his pool cue missing from where he'd set it down before talking with some people. He had no idea who, but someone had stolen it.

The tournament directors announced, "We are missing a cue stick," and then they described it. "It belongs to Manuel Gonzales Jr. If anyone finds it, please return it to his table."

In the meantime, he had to play his match. He was frustrated by the theft and went down three games to zero.

Then, before the next game began, someone came up to him and said, "We found this." It was his pool cue. It was ice cold, he said. Whoever had taken it must have gone straight to their car and stashed it. But when they announced whose it was, the guilt must have gotten to them, and they brought it back in for someone else to find and return.

The whole ordeal focused Dad, and he came back to win four games to three. He finished second in the tournament.

Most of the time when Dad played, though, you'd never see much of a difference in his demeanor whether he was ahead or behind. I didn't see that in most players. You often start to see their emotions getting the better of them. Their body language tells you they're already beaten. They start to show frustration at every miss, you hear them cussing under their breath, or all of their friendliness evaporates. Their demeanor says it all.

To come back when you're down, you've got to really know who you are. If your identity is wrapped up in being a good pool player, then your whole world can fall apart when you play badly. But it's just a game. You've got to find that focus edge. There's a lot more to who we are in life as members of a family, leaders, businesspeople, before God, and among friends. You've got to keep things in perspective.

You've got to remember you're having fun, and fun is about learning and seeing what you can do, not about what you can't. It's no big deal to get beaten, but it's no fun to beat yourself.

It takes courage not to let a moment define you. It's not something many people can do. Too many live in moments as if those moments exemplify them, but we shouldn't limit ourselves to anything that happened in the past—even in the last few seconds. When you approach something as if your performance defines your identity—success or failure—you're living in debt to the past. Instead, like my dad said, you should be living for every next shot and letting the baggage of the past go. If you can do that, then win, lose, or draw, you are improving. Some shots will express your best; others won't. You're still growing.

It's like the serenity prayer I learned when I was growing up that I think of often:

> God, grant me the serenity to accept the
> things I cannot change,
> the courage to change the things I can,
> and the wisdom to know the difference.[21]

To live by that, though, you've got to stop and think. It takes its own habit of keeping perspective.

For me, I absorbed that lesson from watching my dad, but I know he learned it from all he suffered through and overcame during his lifetime. He always carried an air of "Things could be a lot worse," and "This is supposed to be fun. If it's not, let's go do something that is."

You can't change a missed shot, but you can change your next shot. You should consider the attitude you carry into your next shot as more of who you really are than whether you missed or made the last shot.

So don't give up. Don't stop playing one game at a time, one shot at a time, and give your game a chance to come together. It's not easy, and it takes a lot of heart. I shared that with my oldest son, MG4, and on the same night I said that to him, he came back from a really large deficit to win a match. For a moment, I got a glimpse of how proud my dad must have been of me, his son, because I was sure proud of mine.

Learning the Hard Lessons

Michael Lewis's little book *Coach: Lessons on the Game of Life* is about a hard-nosed, competitive coach who molded high schoolers into men using becoming excellent at the game of baseball. In the book, Coach Fitz is the old-school tough coach who drives his players to be their best by driving them to their edge, both physically and mentally. He took baseball seriously because life is serious, and baseball is a microcosm of life.

He used winning, not as the be-all, end-all purpose of the game, but as a measurement of character. Do you have what *it* takes? Mr. Lewis writes, "By 'it' he didn't mean the importance of winning or even, exactly, trying hard.... 'It' was the importance of battling one's way through all the easy excuses life offered for giving up."[22] Coach Fitz was hard, not because he demanded winning at all costs, but because he knew if you could form the qualities necessary to win baseball games, then more than likely you also had the stuff to create a good life for yourself. You could find it in yourself to forgo the easy excuses for quitting when you shouldn't, the stuff that makes champions, good leaders, good parents, and good people.

My dad was certainly no Coach Fitz in intensity, but he instilled the same "no excuses to give up" mentality. He had lost his father before he was a teenager, moved away from friends to Texas and Mexico at a critical time in his life, gotten on that bus to boot camp in July 1967, endured boot camp and a war, and then returned to the States in August 1968, broken in body and spirit. He had certainly given more than one would hope for in a simple life. He could easily have turned into a hard, resentful man who felt cheated by his life circumstances. He could have been a tough-love coach like Fitz, but he chose another way. He exemplified no excuses for living your best life, and he brought the best out of others in his own gentle and playful way by listening, teaching, encouraging, and showing the way in everything he did.

Mr. Lewis's book *Coach* rings with admiration for its main character on every page, despite sharing some of the toughest challenges this coach ran Mr. Lewis and others through as he tried to bring greatness out of them. In the end, you get a sense of tremendous gratitude to the tough coach from the author and many others. Alumni rallied together, after all, to name the school's new gym after him. Mr. Lewis's writing expresses gratitude to Coach Fitz for caring enough to bring the best out of him—to show him some strengths he didn't even know he had—and admiration for a man who loved his players enough to constantly press them beyond their liking. As Mr. Lewis put it, "All I knew was that he cared about the way we played a game in a way we'd never seen anyone care about anything. . . . I recalled a man trying to give boys a sense that their lives could be something other than ordinary."[23]

No, my dad wasn't like Coach Fitz outwardly, but I think many of the lessons he taught me were very similar to what Coach Fitz fought to teach his players. He taught me about excellence through a game he loved, and he used that game over and over again as a metaphor for life. He taught me I could have a good life if I valued the right things and worked hard and smart, and that good could turn to extraordinary if I was grateful for everything it gave me and if I valued God, family, work, and fun.

There was very little hard about my dad. He went through a lot in his life, but bitterness never found any root in him. I credit a lot of that to my mom, who was there for him when he got back from Vietnam and refused to ever believe anything other than that he was the best man in the world for her to have married. That gave him room to become whole. Very seldom do we realize how important others are in our journeys. I know Dad always appreciated Mom for the part she played in his.

A good life doesn't just happen; it's built of moments and how we behave in them. It's built on accepting the challenge to overcome shortcomings or hardships, creating friends and not enemies, and playing it all with grace.

Dad taught me everything I know in business, everything I know in pool, and everything I know about marriage, parenting, and grandparenting. I'll always appreciate him for being my life coach.

Finishing Well

In 2008, Dad was once again at the VNEA International Championships in Las Vegas. Somehow Don Fuller, the man who had saved his life, found out and came down with his wife. Don, his wife, and Mom and Dad met in a restaurant to have a meal together, just like so many others Dad had made friends with over the years. Mom gave Don a twelve-by-sixteen picture of our family from a recent gathering. It was an up-to-date photo of all of my parents' kids, grandkids, and great-grandkids. I believe she wanted Don to see how that life-changing decision he made, to help my dad get to safety, resulted in my dad having such a big, beautiful family. We are all forever grateful for Don's choice that day.

Don Fuller and Dad, the day he thanked Don for saving his life

It was then that Dad got to finally tell Don how glad he was that he didn't die that day. He got to reverse the last words he'd spoken to Don in that hospital room at Củ Chi Base Camp. Had Don not saved him, that picture would have been more than half empty, and there wouldn't be any pool trophies in Mom's basement. There would be a completely different kind of community in the pool halls around Greeley. All that Dad lived, all that he accomplished, all the lives he touched—all of that would never have happened.

The photo of Dad's legacy he gave to Don

For my dad, I know he faced a challenge just getting out of that VA hospital bed to face life again when he felt like an "incomplete" man. There's no question that I will never know the extent of what it was like to wake up from that helicopter ride back to base and discover the nightmare he had just experienced was a reality. He woke up with burns all over his body, a leg and half of his arm gone, and worst of all, the feeling he would have been better off had he not survived. He must have also felt no one could ever love him again.

But that wasn't true. Wholeness has little to do with how many appendages we have. It's a matter of the soul. I've met far more injured individuals in my lifetime, and you could see nothing of it in their physical appearance other than a brokenness of soul in their eyes.

I think life is more like pool than football. It has more to do with how courageously you face what is next than choosing to mope about the mistakes of the past. Sure, you can "put yourself behind the eight ball," but with the right amount of skill and the courage to try, you can spin around the eight ball and sink what's on the other side. It's hard, but not impossible. With enough practice, anyone can learn to master the massé shot you'd need to do that. If not, you can also always jump over it or kick it in. There are always options.

If you're afraid to fail, pool is probably not a game for you, and life can be a tough game as well. In some instances—as in some of the pool games I told you about earlier—to play it safe means never to learn what control you can ultimately have of the cue ball and to never get a chance to grow in the game. You can't play pool—or life—without courage. Each is best approached as a journey where the next step is more important than the last. Both pool and life are best approached with thoughts about where you're going rather than filled with remorse and regret about past mistakes.

In late 2023, I started interviewing my mom and dad with the thought of writing this book, and I got to hear some stories I'd never heard before. I also got to relive some great memories from their perspective rather than my own. My only regret is that I didn't start doing it earlier.

Left to right: Mom, Renee, Dad, me, and Denise

Dad passed away just after the ringing in of the new year in 2024. It was a sad time, but also one when the community he had helped form came together to remember him and commemorate together all that he taught each of us over the years. A lot of what was shared at that time is also reflected in the pages of this book. I know as well, there are more stories out there than could be contained in these pages. Dad lived that kind of full life. He touched the world in that kind of way.

As I look to the future and bring into it the best of the past, I hope to live up to all he hoped for me, my sisters, his grandchildren, and his friends. With his spirit watching over me, I hope to get back into the tournaments again soon, back to playing and sharing the game I know he loved. I hope I can be half the community creator that he was.

Maybe I'll see you at a tournament soon. If you see me, come over and say hi. If you have a story about my dad, I'd love to hear it. If not, I'm glad, at least, that you got to read about him here and how he touched so many lives. Hopefully a little bit will have rubbed off on you as your eyes have run across the words on these pages.

Here's to each of us playing our best game and living our fullest life in the years ahead. I know that's what my dad would have wanted for all of us.

From the VNEA Hall of Fame Website

Manuel Gonzales Jr.
Charter: High Country/TD Rowe –
Fort Collins, Colorado

FROM THE VNEA HALL OF FAME WEBSITE

Manuel is a long-time member of the VNEA and has served as the captain of numerous teams throughout his pool career. He furthers his involvement with the leagues by assisting in local tournament activity and spending time helping others increase their skill level.

In 1994 and 1997, Manuel's Men's A team placed 2nd and 1st, respectively, at the coveted Rocky Mountain Team Tournaments. He also captured 1st place in Open A/AA Singles at the 1996 High Country/TD Rowe 1st Annual Pool Tournament. Since 1970, Manuel has absorbed many local honors.

Like a number of other talented VNEA pool players have done, Manuel has completed the VNEA Certified Referee School and has used his certification to raise the level of professionalism displayed at his local events by promoting accuracy in call making.

> My most memorable moment in the VNEA was in 1997 at the Int'l Championships in Las Vegas when my son Manuel Gonzales III and his team finished first in the Open Team Division.
>
> —Manuel Gonzales Jr.

Notes

[1] "Colorado Hispanic/Latino Historical Overview," HistoryColorado.org, accessed April 15, 2024, https://www.historycolorado.org/colorado-hispanic-latino-historical-overview.

[2] Anna Kennedy, "Auraria (West Denver)," Colorado Encyclopedia.org, accessed April 15, 2024, https://coloradoencyclopedia.org/article/auraria-west-denver.

[3] Gary Keller, *The One Thing: The Surprisingly Simple Truth Behind Extraordinary Results* (Austin, TX: Bard Press, 2012), 9.

[4] Keller, 10.

[5] "For the Love of the Game—Dialogue Transcript," Script-o-rama.com, accessed April 12, 2024, http://www.script-o-rama.com/movie_scripts/f/for-love-of-the-game-script.html.

[6] Trish Long, "Assassination, Torture, Drug Smuggling Fuel History of US-Mexico Border Closing, scrutiny," *El Paso Times*, April 3, 2019, https://www.elpasotimes.com/story/news/2019/04/03/border-closed-after-assassination-president-john-f-kennedy-enrique-kiki-camarena-drug-smuggling/3357101002/.

[7] Terry Brisbane and Rusty Rueff, *The Faith Code: A Future Proof Framework for a Life of Meaning and Impact* (New York: Morehouse Publishing, 2023), 5.

[8] Steven Johnson, *Where Good Ideas Come From: The Natural History of Innovation* (New York: Riverhead Books, 2010), 152–53.

[9] Available on YouTube at https://www.youtube.com/watch?v=J-swZaKN2Ic (or just search "The Power of Yet Carol Dweck").

[10] "Tet Offensive Attack on Tan Son Nhut Air Base," *Wikipedia*, accessed May 9, 2024, https://en.wikipedia.org/wiki/Tet_offensive_attack_on_Tan_Son_Nhut_Air_Base.

[11] Marie Forleo, *Everything Is Figureoutable* (New York: Portfolio, 2019), 3.

[12] Edwin Louis Cole, *Courage: Winning Life's Toughest Battles* (Tulsa, OK: Honor Books, 1991), 41–42.

[13] Robert Waldinger and Marc Schulz, *The Good Life: Lessons from the World's Longest Scientific Study of Happiness* (New York: Simon & Schuster, 2023), 3.

[14] Waldinger and Schulz, *The Good Life*, 21.

NOTES

15 Jordan Peterson, *12 Rules for Life: An Antidote to Chaos* (Toronto: Random House Canada, 2018), 285–86.
16 Cindy Carrillo, *Finding Your Nxt: When You're Ready for the Life You Really Want* (Ridgway, CO: Nxt Publishing, 2023), 36–37.
17 Steven Pressfield, *The War of Art: Break Through the Blocks and Win Your Inner Creative Battles* (New York: Black Irish Entertainment, 2002), xvii–xviii.
18 Vivek H. Murthy, *Together: The Healing Power of Human Connection in a Sometimes Lonely World* (New York: Harper Wave, 2020), xix.
19 Ron Stewart, "Aim Student Shows Skeptics: Manuel Gonzales, Jr.," *Greeley Tribune*, December 18, 1974, 10–11.
20 Richard Carlson, *Don't Sweat the Small Stuff . . . And It's All Small Stuff: Simple Ways to Keep the Little Things from Taking Over Your Life* (New York: Hyperion, 1997), 1–2.
21 The Serenity Prayer is attributed to Reinhold Niebuhr, a Lutheran theologian.
22 Michael Lewis, *Coach: Lessons on the Game of Life* (New York: W.W. Norton & Company, 2005), 54.
23 Lewis, 58, 62.

About the Author

MANUEL GONZALES III is a father, grandfather, entrepreneur, and amateur pool champion. He and his wife, Cassandra, co-founded SSC Doctors, Inc., in 2016. They live in northern Colorado with their children and grandchildren, continuing a tradition of entrepreneurship and pool champions into its fourth generation.

www.ingramcontent.com/pod-product-compliance
Lightning Source LLC
Chambersburg PA
CBHW021146160426
43194CB00007B/713